American Indian Literature and Critical Studies Series
Gerald Vizenor, General Editor

American Gypsy

Also by Diane Glancy

AMERICAN GYPSY

Six Native American Plays

DIANE GLANCY

University of Oklahoma Press : Norman

This is a work of fiction. Names, characters, places, and incidents are either the product of the author's imagination or are used fictitiously, and any resemblance to actual events, locales, or persons, living or dead, is entirely coincidental.

This book is published with the generous assistance of The McCasland Foundation, Duncan, Oklahoma.

LIBRARY OF CONGRESS CATALOGING-IN-PUBLICATION DATA

Glancy, Diane.
    American gypsy : six Native American plays / Diane Glancy.
        p.   cm.   —(American Indian literature and critical
    studies series ; v. 45)
    ISBN 0-8061-3456-9 (hc : alk. paper)
    1. Indians of North America—Drama   I. Title.   II. Series.

PS3557.L294 A84 2002
812'.54—dc21

                                                    2002018870

American Gypsy: Six Native American Plays
is Volume 45 in the American Indian Literature
and Critical Studies Series.

The paper in this book meets the guidelines for permanence and durability of the Committee on Production Guidelines for Book Longevity of the Council on Library Resources, Inc. ∞

1   2   3   4   5   6   7   8   9   10

A stage is suspended in the air. The earth hangs beneath it on cords. As long as the voices last, the cords will not break. But when the voices fail, the earth will fall into the chaos below.

FROM THE CHEROKEE

There is still the belief that story holds things together.

The lives of the people depend upon a stage where words take place.

CONTENTS

PREFACE

I wanted a collection of plays that would reverberate like a collection of short stories. I wanted something that kicked apart yet was *bagged,* having to stay together at least on the bound level.

I wanted the different dramatic voices *paged* together.
I wanted the feel of linked stages.

Script structures the relationship of the actors to the meaning they are responsible for.

It curves along a road of how the actors see their space in lines,
speak back to it,
how they interact with it.

Script defines the relationship of process in the functional aspects of being.
It determines the style of pacing,
the wobbly corridor
which is the carrier of the structure
questioning the meaning the actors find
for their wait by the road.

Script is the arbitrary and interactory process of organizing variables
that resist
and should.

Script makes story of explanation.

It coalesces the array of arbitrary elements into patterns of images upon which the action rides.

American Gypsy

The Woman Who Was a Red Deer Dressed for the Deer Dance

My deer dress is the way I felt,
transformed by the power of ceremony.

The idea for "The Woman Who Was a Red Deer Dressed for the Deer Dance" came from Carolyn Erler's The Crone, a red papier-mache dress, used on this book's cover.

This dramatic/poetic piece is an intermixing of ethnographic material. The story of Ahw'uste was taken from "Doi on Ahu'usti" and "Asudi on Ahw'usti," *Friends of Thunder, Tales of the Oklahoma Cherokees,* edited by Frank and Anna Kilpatrick (University of Oklahoma Press, 1995), pieces of the old language (Cherokee), and contemporary materials (the granddaughter's life in the soup kitchen and dance bars). It is a dialogue/monologue between a grandmother and her granddaughter, each arguing against the other for her own way of life. The grandmother talks about stories and the Spirits and the red-deer dress she has made to feel more in tune with Ahw'uste, a mythological spirit deer. The granddaughter talks about the problems of contemporary life, including her experiences with several men. The grandmother continues talking about Ahw'uste and the Spirits, who in the end, she realizes, let her down. "Damned Spirits," she hits the table with her fist, "didn't always help us out. Let us have it rough sometimes," she says as she talks of hunger and the uncertainty she faced in her life. The granddaughter says she has to look for work, which she can't find, and says she doesn't have time for the Ahw'uste and the Spirits and longs for more practical help from her grandmother. In the end the granddaughter enters some of her grandmother's world, saying, "You know, I've learned she told me more without speaking than she did with her words."

In this I try. Well, I try. To combine the overlapping realities of myth, imagination, & memory with spaces for the silences. To make a story. The voice speaking in different agencies. Well, I try to move on with the voice in its guises. A young woman & her grandmother in a series of scenelets. Divided by a line of flooring. Shifting between dialogue & monologue. Not with the linear construct of conflict / resolution, but with story moving like rain on a windshield. Between differing & unreliable experiences.

GIRL

Have you heard of Ahw'uste?

GRANDMOTHER

I have, but I've forgotten.

GIRL

They said they fed her.

GRANDMOTHER

Yes, they did.

GIRL

What was she?

GRANDMOTHER

I don't know.

GIRL

A deer?

GRANDMOTHER

Yes, a deer. A small deer.

GIRL

She lived in the house, didn't she?

GRANDMOTHER

Yes, she did. She was small.

GIRL

They used to talk about her a long time ago, didn't they?

GRANDMOTHER

Yes, they did.

GIRL

Did you ever see one of the deer?

GRANDMOTHER

I saw the head of one once. Through the window. Her head was small and she had tiny horns.

GIRL

Like a goat?

GRANDMOTHER

Yes, like that.

GIRL

Where did you see her?

GRANDMOTHER

I don't know. Someone had her. I just saw her. That's all.

GIRL
  You saw the head?
GRANDMOTHER
  Yes, just the head.
GIRL
  What did they call her?
GRANDMOTHER
  A small deer.
GIRL
  Where did you see her?
GRANDMOTHER
  What do they call it down there?
GIRL
  Deer Creek.
GRANDMOTHER
  Yes, that's where I saw her.
GIRL
  What did they use her for?
GRANDMOTHER
  I don't know. There were bears there, too. And larger
  deer.
GIRL
  Elk maybe?
GRANDMOTHER
  Yes, they called them elk.
GIRL
  Why did they have them?
GRANDMOTHER
  They used them for medicine.
GIRL
  How did they use them?
GRANDMOTHER
  They used their songs.
GIRL
  The deer sang?
GRANDMOTHER
  No, they were just there. They made the songs happen.

GIRL
   The elk, too?
GRANDMOTHER
   Yes, the elk too.
GIRL
   And the moose?
GRANDMOTHER
   Yes, the moose.

GIRL

   It was like talking to myself when I stayed with her. If I asked her something, she answered flat as the table between us.

   Open your deer mouth and talk. You never say anything on your own. I could wear a deer dress. I could change into a deer like you. We could deer dance in the woods under the redbirds. The bluejays. The finches.

   U-da-tlv:da de-s-gi-ne-hv'-si, E-li'-sin.
   Pass me the cream, Grandmother.
   My cup and saucer on the oilcloth.

   How can you be a deer? You only have two legs.
GRANDMOTHER
   I keep the others under my dress.

GIRL

   It was a wordless world she gave me. Not silent, but wordless. Oh, she spoke, but her words seemed hollow. I had to listen to her deer noise. I had to think what she meant. It was like having a conversation with myself. I asked. And I answered. Well—I could hear what I wanted.

   When I was with her I talked and never stopped, because her silence ate me like buttered toast.

   What was she saying? Her words were in my own hearing?—
   I had to know what she said before I could hear it?

GRANDMOTHER

I don't like this world any more. We're reduced to what can be seen.

GIRL

She fought to live where we aren't tied to table and fork and knife and chair.

It was her struggle against what happens to us.

Why can't you let me in just once and speak to me as one of your own? You know I have to go into the *seeable*— live away from your world. You could give me more.

GIRL

You work the church soup kitchen before? You slop up the place and I get to clean up. You night shifts think you're tough shit. But I tell you, you don't know nothing. I think you took my jean jacket. The one with Jesus on the cross in sequins on the back. Look—I see your girl wearing it—I'll have you on the floor.

Don't think I don't know who's taking the commodities —I'm watching those boxes of macaroni and cheese disappear.

I know it was you who lost the key to the storeroom, and I had to pay for the locksmith to change the lock. They kept nearly my whole check. I couldn't pay my rent. I only got four payments left on my truck. I'm not losing it.

GIRL

She said once, there were wings the deer had when it flew. You couldn't see them, but they were there. They pulled out from the red-deer dress. Like leaves opened from the kitchen table—

Like the stories that rode on her silence. You knew they were there. But you had to decide what they meant.

Maybe that's what she gave me—the ability to fly when I knew I had no wings. When I was left out of the old world that moved in her head. When I had to go on without her stories.

They get crushed in this world.

But they're still there. I hear them in the silence sometimes.

I want to wear a deer dress. I want to deer dance with Ahw'uste—

GIRL

What does *Ahw'uste* mean in English?

GRANDMOTHER

I don't know what the English was. But Ahw'uste was a spirit animal.

GIRL

What does that mean?

GRANDMOTHER

She was only there for some people to see.

GIRL

She was only there when you thought she was?

GRANDMOTHER

She had wings, too. If you thought she did. She was there to remind us—you think you see something you're not sure of. But you think it's there anyway.

GIRL

Maybe Jesus used wings when he flew to heaven. Ascended right up the air. Into Holy Heaven. Floating and unreachable. I heard them stories at church when I worked the soup kitchen.

Or maybe they're wings like the spirits use when they fly between the earth and sky—but when you pick up a spirit on the road, you can't see his wings—he's got them folded into his jacket.

GRANDMOTHER

They say rocket ships go there now.

GIRL

The ancestors?

GRANDMOTHER

Yes, all of them wear red-deer dresses.

GIRL

With two legs under their dresses?

GRANDMOTHER

In the afterworld they let them down.

GIRL

A four-legged deer with wings—wearing a red-deer dress with shoes and hat? Dancing in the leaves—red maple, I suppose? After they're raked up to the sky? Where they stay red forever only if they think they do?—

Sometimes your hooves are impatient inside your shoes. I see them move. You stuff twigs in your shoes to make them fit your hooves. But I know hooves are there.

Why would I want to be a deer like you?
Why would I want to eat without my hands?
Why would I want four feet?
What would I do with a tail? It would make a lump behind my jeans.

Do you know what would happen if I walked down the street in a deer dress?

If I looked for a job?
I already know I don't fit anywhere—I don't need to be reminded—I'm at your house, Grandma, with my sleeping bag and old truck—I don't have anyplace else to go—

GIRL

(*Angrily*) Okay, dude. Dudo. I pick you up on the road. I take you to the next town to get gas for your van, take you back when it still won't start, I pull you to town 'cause you don't have money for a tow truck. I wait two hours while you wait. Buy you supper. I give you love, what do you want? Hey, dude, your cowboy boots are squeaking, your hat with the beaded band. Your CB's talking to the highway, the truckers, the girls driving by themselves—that's what you look for. You take what we got. While you got one eye on your supper, one eye on your next girl.

I could have thought you were a spirit. You could have been something more than a dude—

GRANDMOTHER

The leaves only get to be red for a moment. Just a moment, and then the tree grieves all winter until the leaves come back. But they're green through the summer. The maple waits for the leaves to turn red. All it takes is a few cold mornings. A few days left out of the warmth.

Then the maple tree has red leaves for a short while.

GIRL

(*Angrily*) I can't do it your way, Grandma. I have to find my own trail—Is that why you won't tell me? Is that why you won't speak? I'm caught? I have no way through? But there'll be a way through—I just can't see it yet. And if I can't find it, it's still there. I speak it through. Therefore, it is. If not now, then later. It's coming. If not for me—then for others.

I have to pass through this world not having a place but I'll go anyway.

GRANDMOTHER

That's Ahw'uste.

GIRL

I'll speak these stories I don't know. I'll speak because I don't know them.

GRANDMOTHER

We're the tree waiting for the red leaves.

We count on what's not there as though it is because the maple has red leaves—only you can't always see them.

GIRL

You'd rather live with what you can't see—is that the point of your red-leaf story?

GRANDMOTHER

I was trying to help you over the hard places.

GIRL

I can get over them myself.

GRANDMOTHER

I wanted you to look for the red leaves instead of the dudes on the highway.

GIRL

A vision is *not* always enough—

GRANDMOTHER

It's all I had.

GIRL

You had me—is a vision worth more than me?

GRANDMOTHER

I wanted to keep the leaves red for you.

GIRL

I don't want you to do it for me.

GRANDMOTHER

What am I supposed to do?

GIRL

Find someone else to share your silence with.

GIRL

I was thinking we could have gone for a drive in my old truck.

GRANDMOTHER

I thought we did.

GRANDMOTHER

Ahw'uste's still living. Up there on the hill, straight through *(indicating)* near Asuwosg' Precinct. A long time ago, I was walking by there hunting horses. There was a trail that went down the hill. Now there's a highway on that hill up there, but then, the old road divided. Beyond that, in the valley near Ayohli Amayi, I was hunting horses when I saw them walking and I stopped.

They were this high *(indicating)* and had horns. They were going that direction *(indicating)*. It was in the forest, and I wondered where they were going. They were all walking. She was going first, just this high *(indicating)*, and she had little horns. Her horns were just as my hands are shaped—five points, they call them five points. That's the way it was. Just this high *(indicating)*. And there was a second one, a third one, and a fourth one. The fifth one was huge, and it also had horns with five points. They stopped awhile and they watched me. I was afraid of the large one! They were turning back, looking at me. They were pawing with their feet, and I was afraid. They were showing their anger then. First they'd go *(paw)* with the right hoof and then with the left, and they'd go: *Ti! Ti! Ti! Ti!* They kept looking at me and pawing, and I just stood still.

They started walking again and disappeared away off, and I wondered where they went. I heard my horses over there, and I went as fast as I could. I caught a horse to ride and took the others home.

There was a man named Tseg' Ahl'tadeg and when I got there *(at his house)*, he asked me, what did you see?

I saw something down there, I told him.

What was it?

A deer. She was just this *(indicating)* high, and she had horns like this *(indicating)*, and she was walking in front. The second one was this *(indicating)* high, and the third one was this *(indicating)* high, and the fourth one *(indicating)*—then the rest were large.

It was Ahw'uste, he said.

GIRL

I thought you said Ahw'uste lived in a house in Deer Creek.

GRANDMOTHER

Well, she did, but these were her tribe. She was with them sometimes.

GIRL

She's the only one who lived in a house?

GRANDMOTHER

Yes.

GIRL

In Deer Creek?

GRANDMOTHER

Yes, in Deer Creek.

GIRL

Your deer dress is the way you felt when you saw the deer?

GRANDMOTHER

When I saw Ahw'uste, yes. My deer dress is the way I felt, transformed by the power of ceremony. The idea of it in the forest of my head.

GIRL

Speak without your stories. Just once. What are you without your deer dress? What are you without your story of Ahw'uste?

GRANDMOTHER

We're carriers of our stories and histories. We're nothing without them.

GIRL

We carry ourselves. Who are you besides your stories?

GRANDMOTHER

I don't know—no one ever asked.

GIRL

Okay, Bucko. I find out you're married. But not living with her. *You aren't married in your heart,* you say. *It's the same as not being married.* And you got kids, too? Yeah, several, I'm sure. Probably left more of them behind to take care of themselves than you admit. You think you can dance me backwards around the floor, Bucko?

GRANDMOTHER

Why would I want to be like you?

GRANDMOTHER

Why can't my granddaughter wait on the spirit? Why is she impatient? It takes awhile sometimes. She says— *Hey, spirit, what's wrong? Your wings broke down? You need a jumper cable to get them started?*

My granddaughter wants to do what she wants. Anything that rubs against her, well, she bucks. Runs the other way. I'm not going to give her my deer dress to leave in a heap on some dude's floor. It comes from long years from my grandmother—

I have to live so far away from you. Take me where you are—I feel the pull of the string (she touches her breastbone). Reel me in. Just pull. I want out of here. I want to see you, ancestors. Not hear the tacky world. No more.

GIRL

You always got your eye on the next world.

GRANDMOTHER

I sit by the television, watch those stupid programs.

GIRL

What do you want? Weed the garden. Do some beans for supper. Set a trap for the next spirit to pass along the road.

GRANDMOTHER

The spirits push us out so we'll know what it's like to be without them. So we'll struggle all our lives to get back in—

GIRL

Is that what life is for you? No—for me—I get busy with day-to-day stuff until it's over.

I told 'em at church I didn't take the commodities—well, not all those boxes—I told 'em—shit—what did it matter?

Have you ever lost one job after another?

GRANDMOTHER

Have you eaten turnips for a week? Because that was all you had in your garden? In your cupboard? Knowing your commodities won't last, because you gave them to the next family on the road? They got kids and you can hear them crying.

GIRL

Well, just step right off the earth. That's where you belong. With your four deer feet.

GRANDMOTHER

Better than your two human ones.

All you do is walk into trouble.

GIRL

Because I pick up someone now and then?

Didn't you know what it was like to want love?

GRANDMOTHER

Love—ha! I didn't think of that. We had children one after another. We were cooking supper or picking up some crying child or brushing the men away. Maybe we did what we didn't want to do. And we did it every day.

GIRL

Well, I want something more for my life.

GRANDMOTHER

A trucker dude or two to sleep with till they move on? Nights in a bar? The jukebox and cowboys rolling you over?

GIRL

(*She slaps her grandmother.*) What did I do? Slap my grandmother?

You deserved it. Sitting there with your smug spirits. I don't curl up with stories. I live in the world I see.

I've got to work.

Christ—where am I going to find another job?
GRANDMOTHER
You can't live on commodities alone.
GIRL
You can't drive around all day in your spirit-mobile.

GIRL

I been paying ten years on my truck, Bub. You think I need a new transmission? 'Cause I got 180,000 miles on the truck and it's in the garage? You think you can sell me a new one, Bubby? My truck'll run another 100,000. I don't have it paid for yet. You think you can sell me a used truck? You couldn't sell me mud flaps. Just get it running —try something else and my grandma'll stomp you with her hooves. My truck takes me in a vision. You got a truck that has visions? I don't see it on the list of options.

GRANDMOTHER
Gu'-s-di i-da-da-dv-hni My relatives—
I'm making medicine from your songs. Sometimes I feel it. But mostly I have to know it's there without seeing. I go there from the hurts he left me with, all those kids and no way to feed them but by the spirit. Sometimes I think the birds brought us food. Or somehow we weren't always hungry. That's not true. Mostly we were on our own. Damned spirits. Didn't always help out. Let us have it rough sometimes. All my kids are gone. Run off. One of my daughters calls from Little Falls sometimes. Drunk. Drugged. They all have accidents. One got shot.

What was that? *E-li'-sin*—Grandmother?

—No, just the bluejay. The finch.

Maybe the ancestors—I hear them sometimes—out there
raking leaves—or I hear them if I think I do.

Hey—quiet out there, my granddaughter would say.

Just reel me in, grandmother, I say.

GIRL

So I told 'em at my first job interview—no, I hadn't
worked that kind of machine—but I could learn.

I told 'em at my second interview the same thing—

I told 'em at the third—

At the fourth I told 'em—
My grandmother was a deer. I could see her change
before my eyes. She caused stories to happen. That's
how I knew she could be a deer.

At the fifth I continued—I'm sewing my own red-deer
dress. It's different than my grandma's. Mine is a dress
of words.
I see Ahw'uste also.

At the rest of the interviews I started right in—Let me
talk for you—that's what I can do.

My grandma covered her trail. Left me without knowing how to make a deer dress. Left me without covering.
But I make a covering she could have left me if only she
knew how.

I think I hear her sometimes—that crevice you see
through into the next world. You look again, it's gone.

My heart has red trees.
The afterworld must be filling up with leaves.

You know, I've learned she told me more without speaking than she did with her words.

The Women Who Loved House Trailers

The Treaty of Structure Can Be Broken.
It's History's Lesson.

Take the existing structure of conflict/resolution. Destruct the text/subtext it saying: brokenness is the first act. Tell the story of a house trailer that is an indigenous construct. Take its shifting placement. Camp it on your own campground regrounded.

Then Look Up

The Native play is a bird with several wings. It's oral tradition told with more than one voice. Told with several voices where one could not go on without the other. I would say a play is a story that the characters enter. No, a play is the characters a story enters.

A canoe of a story
A blow torch of a story
A story of a story

A woman named Siouxsan Monson visited me. Somewhere in our conversation, she mentioned that her grandfather, or great uncle, or perhaps another relative, had made the first house trailer—literally, a tent on wheels—in 1932. I began associating the concept of travel with tepee, migration, portability, a turtle with a house on its back—then I thought of our stories, our families, our roots, our being also as *mobility*. I began thinking of a triad of women telling the movable stories of their lives. The images all came from different places —an art gallery in Provincetown, Massachusetts, where I saw a woven birch-bark canoe in a gallery; a trip to Finland, Australia; the edge of the lake at Quartz Mountain in Oklahoma, where I sat watching little waves coming into the shore and saw them weaving the leaves on a branch of a weeping willow hanging in the water. I also have a colleague at the college where I teach who is a welder. I remember asking her what it felt like to weld.

In looking for a different way to *tellstory*, I turned a piece of drama inside out so only a few strands of plot showed, like one of those sweaters, when you turn it over you can't see the pattern. I knew the plot would be a thin line on which stories from different continents were stranded or hung.

I wanted to take a blade of plot and hang stories from several continents upon it. I wanted to see how far it would (could) sag. I wanted to strand several elements of different stories. I wanted to see how thin I could pull the plot they hung on. I wanted to take several ways of saying the same thing.

The house trailers are three women who come to terms with themselves.

The house trailers are their roaming hearts.

The house trailers are their broken families, whom they learn to accept.

The house trailers are the moving stories of their different lives.

The house trailers are the cultures of several continents, which is another addition to the multidimensional aspect of the new-wave oral tradition I'm trying to create, which is interlocking cultures.

The house trailers are also the problems and limitations of the three women, which are made portable, and some of them, anyway, rolled away.

With love and blow-kisses from the welder's torch.

CHARACTERS

OSCAR
A welder.
JELLY
A weaver of strips of birch bark into small canoes.
BERTA
A collector of stories.

SECTION 1
The Three Women Are Nearing the Last Days in Their
Studio Because We Can't Pay the Rent
SECTION 2
In the Cemetery at Oscar's Father's Funeral
SECTION 3
The Letters or Correspondence
SECTION 4
The Pack Up
SECTION 5
Berta's Uncle's Place / The House Trailer & Road

SECTION 1

The Three Women Are Nearing the Last Days in Their Studio Because *We Can't Pay the Rent.*

BERTA

My grandfather made the *first* house trailer. When I tell my stories, I think of him.

OSCAR

The first time I held a blowtorch I was the sun.
I lowered my welder's mask—
I faced my solar storms.

JELLY

The first canoe I made looked like a crooked quarter-moon. I just kept weaving.

BERTA

My grandpa and his brother made the house trailer. It was a tent on a trailer they could put up and tie down when they moved. There were two benches. They could sit across from one another. After my grandma died, Grandpa drove around with his kids. I guess he didn't know what else to do. My father said all the kids rode in the backseat in the car, the trailer rattling behind them. The car was hot and cramped as they jostled against one another, and the trailer would break down over railroad tracks and bumps. Half the time my father said he was sick. Throwing up in the backseat as his father rolled over the dirt roads. They'd find a lake and fish or just stay in the woods. All they had was an old car and a handmade house trailer.

JELLY

They were turtles with their house on their back.

BERTA

Sometimes, Howdy, his dog, would ride in the backseat with the kids, panting and drooling.

JELLY
> I told Berta the *first* trailer was the tepee folded up and
> dragged on a travois behind a horse.

BERTA
> He made the house trailer from a dream.
> I'm sending off my dream in a grant proposal.
> Leaving it for the mailman.

OSCAR
> A trailer can't go anywhere on its own, that's my first
> objection.

BERTA
> Dreams are hard to work out.

OSCAR
> Berta's the house trailer. It takes us to pull her.

BERTA
> Oscar welds with the fire and brimstone her father
> preached.

OSCAR
> Let Berta tell her stories to herself.

BERTA
> What does Oscar know about telling stories?

OSCAR
> My mother was a wren.
> She made a nest from her anger and discontent.
> Sometimes she was impatient to fly—
> the wings under her dress would move.
> No one could watch anything else.
> Sometimes she chirped.
> Why did you do that, Mother?
> I didn't have friends. I didn't have you.
>
> A wren's nest is a pygmy skull. An upside-down skull.
> A shrunken head.
>
> I had to call her, *queen of the wrens.*
> We made bird food from thistle, cracked corn, sun-
> flower, peanut hearts, millet, safflower.
> She called the wrens *the adored ones of the universe.*

We sat in the backyard in winter like the birds.
She let the snow cover us.

I want a savior who's a blowtorch.
I want to blast day and night.

JELLY

Oscar, queen of the welding school.

OSCAR

Sometimes I dream of the eastern bluebird and house
sparrow, the brown thrasher and red-bellied woodpecker.
The starling, grackle, grosbeak, junco—

The kids chirped at me when I passed.

JELLY

We live in a small skull carried on the stick of the
backbone.

OSCAR

Mother, why didn't you listen?
Why didn't you open your wren-ears and hear?
What did you have to chirp about?

She grilled me on the birds.
I had to repeat—*the wren is queen of them all.*

JELLY

Once I saw a waterlogged boat. I saw how the sinking
boat cradled the water that was sinking it—I saw its ten-
derness—I cupped my hand like a boat—Sometimes I
think of Moses in the bulrushes. I think of nests and
cradles—whatever floats. My eye is trapped by the
woven. I weave the strips of birch bark into a boat and
hang it from the ceiling like a hammock. Sometimes I sit
by the lake and watch the waves among the willow
branches hanging in the water.

OSCAR

I could weld those strips into a metal canoe.

BERTA

I could weave my stories into wings—

JELLY

I had a stepmother. I called her Aunt Arctica.

There was a star in the sky—

in the northern constellation—Arcturus.
Sometimes I dreamed she was my mother.
Sometimes I reached my hand to her.

My first canoes were ice caps.
They were for my stepmother.
I wove the wind and pushed her out to sea.

But Arcturus sparkled up there in the distance.

BERTA

You see the cradle of a story goes anywhere. It crosses the ice field of the heart. It weaves the loose strips together.

I wanted a grandmother. I pretended she was a tree. In the night I hear her leaves rustle. I make a story as if she came to me alone.

OSCAR

The kids chirped at me when I passed.

BERTA

If Jelly could just sell one of her birch bark canoes.

JELLY

If Oscar could sell one of her welded pieces.

OSCAR

Nobody will buy Berta's words.

JELLY

If I was still with Edgar, we could stay with him.

BERTA

My stories are my house trailers.

JELLY

I never knew what Edgar wanted.

BERTA

I never knew what my mother wanted. She cooked and cleaned, and I don't think I ever knew.

Once there was a land called Gondwana—It was Antarctica, Africa and South America before they drifted apart. When we could walk from here to there and didn't need a canoe—Before the willow leaves had water to dip into.

OSCAR

A wing is a story with a canoe.

JELLY

A canoe is a wing with a story.

BERTA

A story is a canoe with a wing.

JELLY

I want to float.

BERTA

I want to talk.

OSCAR

The wren is queen of them all.

JELLY

My stepmother ran the house like an Indian boarding school. I got smacked if I spoke my own language. I thought I had to self-destruct to leave.

Now my weaving speaks my words.

OSCAR

I think my mother would have studied birds. She would have been an ornithologist. Or maybe she just wanted to fly out of there.

BERTA

I want my stories to float like canoes. Fly like wings. Words are my love. The husband of my life. You can hold a word. You can kiss a word as it leaves your mouth.

JELLY

When Edgar left, I knew I'd never love again—I'd have other relationships. I wouldn't be alone. But I wouldn't feel the same about a man—ever. I could fold my blue dancing dress and crush my corsage in a book.

BERTA

I couldn't tell you the times I've been in love—But soon as I felt that way—I'd be looking for someone else—

JELLY

How to live without part of your heart—that's what I'd have to do.

In the Cemetery at Oscar's Father's Funeral

OSCAR
  My father was a minister. If my mother spoke, he quoted
  the Bible. I will multiply your sorrow, Genesis 3:16—

  She finally chirped from the little birdhouse of her head.
BERTA
  Sometimes I feel like I can't get my jacket off—the zip-
  per's stuck. I try to lift the jacket over my head but still
  can't get it off.
JELLY
  Berta's a turtle trying to shed its shell.
OSCAR
  My shell is my welder's helmet.
  Look—the whole family's here—
  their heads float before me like the sea.
  I could be a canoe like Jelly.
  I could blowtorch my way out of the cemetery—
BERTA
  We're like the story of Gondwana, after the continents
  drifted apart. They were all one but had to go their sep-
  arate ways. They couldn't afford their studio rent. The
  earth is always moving apart. What other way have we
  got to go?
JELLY
  The earth is a house trailer, pulled around the sun.
OSCAR
  I think I hated my father. Sometimes at church, he'd have
  his hand on my shoulder as if he was my loving father.
  I had to stand there by him.

  I can't be touched by men. I have a blowtorch. I kiss the
  metal with my fire. I'm working on some metal pieces
  called "The Wren Series." I love the fireworks I make.
  This canal of flames. This chariot. This blast.

BERTA

Oscar can't love because of the father she had.

OSCAR

I can love welding because of the father I had.

JELLY

Oscar, you could love.

OSCAR

Look at his coffin. He's in the *last* house trailer.

JELLY

He doesn't want anything now.

BERTA

I don't know what my mother wanted. She never had the chance to say what she wanted.

JELLY

I don't know what my father wanted. He had the chance but he never said either. He just worked, and I knew he'd buy the bicycle or doll I wanted.

I wish I could find someone like him.

Someone like him who talked.

Someone who said what he wanted.

BERTA

Once a man had a wife who had a baby, and the baby crawled away from the campfire while the wife cooked, and a snake bit the baby, and the baby died. The woman got scared because she was supposed to watch the baby, and she hid it in the bushes. The man came back from hunting and asked where the baby was. The woman said she didn't know. The man found the dead baby in the bushes and stabbed his wife with his spear and threw her in the campfire and burned her to ashes.

OSCAR

My father got away before I could slap his hand off my shoulder. Before he knew how it felt.

Mary Ozbek. Oscar Ozbek. The daughter of Reverend Ozbek.

No. I wanted his touch. I wanted a father.

JELLY

My father couldn't find a woman to love. I know he tried
with my mother. I don't think he loved my stepmother
either. She wouldn't let us talk about our mother. She
sent us to school with a lunch that was like eating a
cloud. It's hard to live with another woman's children
you don't want.

OSCAR

I never had a chance to talk to him.

I was welded in a box.

JELLY

We were in her way. She just couldn't love us.

BERTA

Our families are the house trailers we pull.

OSCAR

Cast down imagination, II Corinthians 10:5, my father
preached. Can you imagine?

JELLY

When my father died, his mouth was shaped like he was
calling my mother's name. At his funeral I expected him
to speak. My stepmother sat in the chair beside me,
though she didn't want to. She got up as soon as it was
over. I knew I was out of the house, though it was my
father's. I climbed in my window and packed my stuff.
Edgar helped. I stayed at his place for awhile, but soon
I could tell he didn't want me either. I got my own place
and he'd come over. But after awhile, he was gone.

OSCAR

I wanted to be bread and my father made me a stone.

I wanted a gift and he gave me what I didn't want.

I took that stone and broke myself. Imagination came
out. He gave me what he wouldn't have if he'd given
me bread.

JELLY

I went back to see Edgar once.

I felt as if a knife had cut us apart.

Once I went back to where my father was born. There was nothing there—No, I felt him there.

OSCAR

You willed him there.

JELLY

I wove him there.

OSCAR

I welded him there.

BERTA

I told stories of him there.

JELLY

Edgar, I ask, how far does a lantern shine in the dark without you? If I can find a postcard stamp. The trailer is in blossom.

Love, Jelly

OSCAR

Write another postcard, Jelly. Sign it, *love and blow kisses from the welder's torch.*

JELLY

Women carry anger and discontent.

BERTA

It's why we're house trailers—

OSCAR

Look at his grave. I'll interrupt my "Wren Series" and weld a heavy piece to hold him there.

JELLY

I could have stayed with Edgar.

OSCAR

I told you to send him downriver.

JELLY

Where does love come from? I want to return it.

Section 3

The Letters or Correspondence

OSCAR

Dear Mary "Oscar" Ozbek, While your "sculpt-piece," as you call it, is interesting, it's large, too large for our space. Could you reduce it, de-wing it in other words?
Love, Holman Gallery

We need studio rent.
I fire the metal wings in half. Leave them ragged.

I name the piece, "Wren w/2 half-wings."

I apply for a grant.
Dear Mary Ozbek. We are sorry to inform you.

I am blown off the earth. Shot through space. My face burns with solar flames.

I have a dream. I am on a table hosed down with cold water because I'm in flames. My body's jerking.

BERTA

My father said he remembers the kids crying in the back-seat over the bumpy roads.

JELLY

—and getting sick.

BERTA

I want a spread of stickers on my bumper from the places we've been. I like to be packed up. Ready to go. I just never know where.

OSCAR

The queen is wren of them all.

JELLY

We could have a house trailer for a studio. Oscar could work on a "Roadside Series." Berta's still got a car. We could hook a drop-top trailer to it.

BERTA

Something like my grandfather made—

OSCAR

Just so we're moving. I want to be far away. Remote.
Distant and unreachable.

BERTA

Once a man had a wife he kept in a bungalow. He was
gone all day and at night came back. He wanted dinner.
He wanted bed. Then he left the next day. The woman was
angry in the bungalow. Her anger was violet. She stormed
at the children. Raged. Blew them out like candles. They
sat as lifeless sacks when the man came home at night.
Where are they? he asked, and bounced them on his knee.
He blew his air into them. They gasped at his used air.
They said, Wow Dad, you gave me what I don't want. But
you give me. That's more than she can do. Yet Mother is
a mother, and I'll say I had a mother and father, and they
did some awkward dance on the bare wood floor of the
bungalow. The chimney rocked. The walls quivered. And
there was some meatloaf and mashed potatoes. There was
a border of flowers high on the wall of the living room.
Just under the ceiling. A jumping-off point. We tried to
climb up there. We had a rope that swings that high. We
hit the lamp and it blew over. We got enraged by Mother.
Where are the children? the man asked when he came in
at night. I don't know, she said. He ate his dinner and hit
her for not making stories of where the children were.
They're in the border of the ceiling, she said. They're up
there in the dead box.

JELLY

I weave canoes that don't float.

I use birch bark because the layers have to be pulled
apart.

Oscar and Berta say my canoes crowd the studio—
Oscar with her large pieces of metal.
Berta with her huge stories.

I hung a canoe near the ceiling after I heard Oscar's
bird stories.

That would make room.

"Canoe in flight," I call it.

Then I hung a canoe upright.

"Returning the Tree" is its name.

OSCAR

Dear Oscar Ozbek, We regret that we've decided against "Wren w/2 half-wings."

BERTA

Is it true, Jelly, Indians can change their name?

OSCAR

Maybe I'll sign my work Ozcar.

BERTA

Jelly will get over Edgar. When she does, I'll name her Jolly.

I'll name myself Birda—because of Oscar's mother, who thought she was a wren.

OSCAR

But my name is Mary Ozbek, not Oscar or Ozcar. Jelly is Joan Hastings, not Jelly or Jolly. Berta is Roberta Hoover—

JELLY

We are three in one.

BERTA

We are one in three.

OSCAR

We are moving out of our studio.

JELLY

Reindeer herders had portable houses—only they were sleds. They were made of reindeer skin or bark—The reindeer pulled them. They were called *ballacks*, I think. They were the *first* house trailers.

OSCAR

If my father had preached, *the Bible was the first house trailer,* I might have listened.

JELLY

Edgar and I went to Finland on our last trip. The first day, I bought a book of folk stories for Berta. I carried it three weeks in my backpack. Later I weighed it. The book was 9½ pounds. I carried it up and down the steps of trains and stations. I lifted it into luggage racks. I carried it onto crowded buses and up and down the stairs and narrow hallways to the rooms where we stayed.

BERTA

Why can't I pay for a studio where I work on my words?

OSCAR

How do I pack my solar storms? How do I move fire?

JELLY

How do I carry my canoes?

BERTA

My stories carry me.

JELLY

Then I'll load my canoes on your words.

BERTA

Mother, why didn't you leave me on a steep shore?
Why didn't you throw me in the sea?
The sea would have found me a husband.
The fish would have given me a wedding.

OSCAR

How do I move the weight of my anger?

BERTA

All we've got are stories. That's where love comes from.

SECTION 4

The Pack Up

BERTA

Once there were three sisters called Meehni, Wimlah, and Gunnedoo who lived with their witch doctor father in the Katoomba tribe in the Jameison Valley of the Blue Mountains in eastern Australia. Their only fear was the Bunyip who lived in a hole. Whenever their father had to pass the hole, he left his daughters on a mountain ledge. One day when he left them, a stone rolled over the ledge into the valley and woke the Bunyip. The angry Bunyip climbed to the three sisters. When the witch doctor saw the Bunyip close to his daughters, he pointed his magic bone at the girls and turned them into stones. The Bunyip chased the witch doctor, who turned himself into a bird. As he flew away, he dropped his magic bone. After the Bunyip had gone, the witch doctor searched for his bone to turn Meehni, Wimlah, and Gunnedoo back into his daughters, but he couldn't find the bone. They were stuck there on the mountain ledge. You can hear the witch doctor, the bird, calling his daughters in search of the bone.

JELLY

We're like those sisters turned into rocks, looking for the magic bone.

OSCAR

My father would say, even the stones could speak, Luke 19:40.

BERTA

Once there were the sisters who loved three brothers from a forbidden tribe. When the brothers rode into the Katoomba camp with their war cries, the father of the girls turned them into rocks but was killed before he could turn them back into girls. When you look at the

Three Sisters Rocks across the valley on Echo Point, you can hear the wind saying, *Turn into girls again. Your father's not coming back. How long are you going to wait?*

JELLY

I'd wait for Edgar—

OSCAR

I could weld Edgar in place for Jelly.

JELLY

Berta's got several versions of the same story.

OSCAR

Berta's got several stories of the same version.

BERTA

My uncle has a place he'll let us work. There's room for Jelly's canoes and Oscar's metal.

There's room for my stories.

OSCAR

Once my father made a trip to Africa to preach. I asked him, how did he know the sky would be there? The clouds? The blue air—the light—the rain—the birds? What if there's just empty land with nothing flying above it?

The earth is round as the wheel of a house trailer. But does the sky cover the whole earth?

My father said, He spreads the heavens like a tent, Isaiah 40:22.

I wanted him to talk to me, but he quoted the Bible.

JELLY

My father said, my mother thought if a bird got into your house, someone would die. My stepmother laughed.

BERTA

My grandfather wasn't satisfied with the sky over him. He hanged a tarp on a trailer bed to cover my father, my aunts and uncles.

JELLY

The house trailers are stories of different continents.

BERTA

The house trailers are our roaming hearts.

JELLY

The foot of a bird is a root pulled loose from the earth.

OSCAR

I've had correspondence with a dream.

I'm working on a smaller piece, "The Wren Garden."

Then I'll work on the heavier piece for my father's
grave. I'll call it, "The Burial Mound." It will hold him
under the ground.

JELLY

You walk through a dream with your birch bark canoe.

OSCAR

You walk through a dream with your blowtorch.

BERTA

You walk through a dream with your stories as you close
the studio door behind you.

SECTION 5

Berta's Uncle's Place /
The House Trailer & Road

BERTA

My uncle doesn't know what happened to the *first* house trailer Grandpa Hoover made. He doesn't want to know.

We work at his place.

Jelly catalogs her canoes. She sells one to a cafe in Cloquet. They hang it from the ceiling.

Oscar has a showing of her "Wren Series" in Duluth. My uncle is a surveyor. She works with him sometimes. They travel in his Landrover.

JELLY

You are given any moment. You want to know what it's like. I say, let the waves come under me.

OSCAR

My new work is called, "The American Roadside Series":
I name a piece:
"Wren-house w/3 wings flying through a field."
I name another piece:
"Bird in the House."

JELLY

Not that, Oscar.

OSCAR

I could hold a blowtorch to my head.

JELLY

What's she doing? She'll torch herself!

BERTA

You can't do that, Oscar. You'll fizzle your hair.

JELLY

Get the torch, Berta.

OSCAR

Let me up.

BERTA

Not until you let go of the blowtorch.

OSCAR

Why would I want to fry myself?—I've got everything
going—

BERTA

I'll tell you a story, Oscar. It will hold you above the
ground.

Words are medicine for a journey. Once the Indians sang
to the sun as it sank in the sky to pass through the under-
world at night. But it's the sun that stays in one place.
It's us who pass through the dark in our dreams.

JELLY

Hold on, Oscar—Get hooked up again to the world—

OSCAR

A dream is a house trailer.

JELLY

If Edgar came right now
I'd snatch a kiss from his mouth
though he bit me like a wolf.
I would touch him on the hand
though a snake were in his palm.

BERTA

A long time ago there were no horses, but some of the
people started having dreams. They saw the horses—the
manes and tails. They knew just how the horses would
look. They made some horses out of mud. They gave
them water to drink. They put them in good grass. They
spoke words to them. One day they went to the meadow
and the horses were alive.

JELLY

Let Oscar weld a travois to the horses.

BERTA

Let Jelly weave a birdhouse.

JELLY

Let Berta tell a story that sounds like a house trailer on the road.

OSCAR

I could weld a bigger wren house. Put it on wheels. I name my "Roadside Series" piece, "Pulling the Birdhouse."

JELLY

I could put a wheel on my canoe.

I could hang the canoe with a wheel from the ceiling.

BERTA

Jelly could call her piece, "The Birchbark Wheelbarrow."

OSCAR

I drive through my solar storms.

JELLY

At night, my canoes twink up there like the stars.

OSCAR

On the road, I see my flame as a headlight from my welder's gun.

*Charlie and B. F. Hoover in their house trailer, circa 1932.
Photo courtesy Siouxson Monson.*

"He made the house trailer from a dream." Photo courtesy Siouxson Monson.

American Gypsy

An American Gypsy is a Native American who knows migration and rootlessness.

The one-act play is in fourteen sections. The sections are tableaus against a barren, pastel landscape, maybe a washed-out orange light against a stark back wall.

In the evening there are stars in the night sky.

The sections of the play move between a house on a dead-end road near Anadarko, Oklahoma, a shed near the house where some boxes are stored, a cemetery with a variety of various-shaped stones across the road, a brief section in Neville's Café, and a dirt road by the chicken farm.

It is Labor Day and a few days following.

Maybe it's the play that is the gypsy.

Peri and Frennie are sisters. Frennie's name is also Chicken Baby, because sometimes there is a possibility of shape changing.

When Peri's husband, TiToMo, is killed during a joy shooting by a bullet shot into the air and returned to earth with enough velocity to lodge in his brain (which I actually read about in the newspaper), Ti's biker friends gather for a dispersal of dialogue. Then Peri is a widow with William on her tail. She wants to open a bed-and-breakfast and use her love of cooking.

I've always loved Gabriel García Márquez's story, "A Very Old Man with Enormous Wings." *American Gypsy* is about migration and finding roots after the migration is over. But Frennie remembers an old story of what happens to Indians when they turn white. They grow feathers and become chickens.

CHARACTERS

PERI

A mixed-blood woman nearing forty.

FRENNIE

Peri's younger sister.

TITOMO (pronounced *Tie-toe-moe* with a stress on the first syllable)

Peri's husband, age forty-three. He's still in love with his wife, though he's not able to understand her at the moment.

WILLIAM, NEVILLE, AND REEP

TiToMo's friends, who think a lot of him and Peri and hang around the pleasure of their company, though their impatience shows when the couple's troubles grow turbulent. Neville owns a cafe where Peri works. Reep drives a beer truck. William is an oil-field worker with TiToMo, both of whose jobs are threatened. They all suffer from a growing awareness that their lives aren't the same as they used to be. They wear old jeans and T-shirts. They are a mix of various tribes.

(OCHOLEE

Peri's friend, who is dead, is pronounced *O-cho-lee*, with a stress on the first syllable, and *cho* with a long *o* as in *choke*. Two other friends who are dead: *FIFT*, with long *i* like *fight*, and *CHUNE*, with a hard *ch* like *Chuck*.)

*"He's an angel," she told them. "He must have
been coming for the child, but . . . the rain knocked
him down."*

GABRIEL GARCÍA MÁRQUEZ,
"A VERY OLD MAN WITH ENORMOUS WINGS"

✳

*And it came to pass, as they fled . . . the Lord
cast down stones from heaven upon them . . .
and they died.*

JOSHUA 10:11

SECTION 1

Peri, William and Frennie are on the front porch. TiToMo, Neville, and Reep are in the cemetery, joy shooting into the air with their pistols. It is afternoon.

FRENNIE

> It sounds like thunder—

PERI

> It's TiTo and his friends shooting off their guns in the cemetery.

The sound of another pistol. Frennie covers her ears. Peri holds her.

FRENNIE

> Once in the barnyard, the lightning came into the chicken house when we were at Aunt Julia's. Remember, Peri—it rolled along the perch. The hens laid eggs for days.

> Angels came to the chicken yard and blessed us when we stayed at Aunt Julia's.

PERI

> Frennie—you should be home—I thought Mom was at your place.

FRENNIE

> I left after she did.

PERI

> You're going to lose another husband.

FRENNIE

> He went to the reservoir.

WILLIAM

> Frennie lives too near that chicken farm. Her husband should be looking for another house.

FRENNIE

> I wanted to come to Aunt Julia's.

WILLIAM

> This isn't Julia's house anymore. It belongs to Peri and TiTo. Aunt Julia is in the cemetery.

PERI

So is my husband.

WILLIAM

But TiTo will be back.

The sound of another pistol.

PERI

You think so? *(Frennie holds her hands to her ears again.)* It's all right, Frennie. The guys are just cutting loose. Maybe TiTo is still getting over his mother's death. *(Peri holds Frennie.)* Frennie could have laid eggs after she thought the lightning rolled into the chicken house.

FRENNIE

Chickens are the angels of the world, Peri. Chickens are pure and white. Remember the hen we chased to death?

Frennie leans against Peri, still holding her ears.

PERI

She was born Chicken Baby. We called her that. Her body was covered with white down. My mother thought she'd die. But Aunt Julia prayed and Frennie lived. The down turned to fuzz. You can only see it if she stands in a light. Sometimes I'd see Frennie with a chicken head. And chicken feet. Sometimes my friend, Ocholee, and I would glue on feathers and chicken dance for her. Sometimes Frennie's fingernails turned under like claws.

WILLIAM

I wish your feet would turn backward. I'd be there for you.

PERI

I wish you'd married Frennie, William. Reep didn't do her any good.

WILLIAM

It was you, Peri.

PERI

Well, I was married to TiTo by the time you figured that out.

FRENNIE

Sometimes a chicken gets into my head and pecks.

PERI

I didn't help Frennie much either. Sometimes I'd see her eat dirt. Sometimes I could feel that little bone in her arm like cartilage in a wing. Aunt Julia prayed for us in the gospel church. We could fly in her visions. I think sometimes it was her vision that turned Frennie white. I thought sometimes, William, I'd die from the light.

SECTION 2

William, Peri, and Frennie are on the porch. TiToMo, Neville, and Reep have returned from the cemetery and are on the steps of the porch and in the yard.

REEP

How can you live down here at the end of the road—catercorner to a graveyard, TiTo?

TITOMO

This house belonged to Julia Halex—Peri's aunt. Peri and Frennie liked to come here when they were girls. I wanted the house too—my parents were always moving—my father was stationed in the east. No, the cemetery doesn't bother me—the stones are like grazing sheep—

WILLIAM

Just like being without our jobs don't bother us. Laborers without labor on Labor Day.

NEVILLE

Those stones look like tepees to me.

WILLIAM

Whatever gets into your head—

TITOMO

Look at William there with my wife. Let's go back to the cemetery—take him joy shooting—

NEVILLE

Whatever gets into your head you can't get out—

PERI

If the sheriff sees you with those guns—

TITOMO

He's at the reservoir today. They're all out there fishing.

REEP

I saw Frennie's husband go by with his rods in his truck.

PERI

TiTo, you'll hurt someone.

NEVILLE

Probably himself.

TITOMO
I'll just shoot the stars up there—
PERI
They aren't out yet.
TITOMO
The stars are up there. You just can't see them.
REEP
Wait till you can't make payments on your house—
you'll be traveling again.
PERI
I don't understand why we have to make house pay-
ments. This house belonged to my Aunt Julia.
TITOMO
The bank owns the house, Peri. Your father sold the
house to pay Aunt Julia's bills. She was sick a long time.
Then there was her funeral. Now the bank owns the
house, and we make monthly payments to the bank.
REEP
Sounds easy to understand—
PERI
What have you ever owned that you know about buy-
ing anything?
REEP
My car. My bike—nearly. Peri's always got her knife and
fork in.
TITOMO
Reep isn't over being married to Frennie.
REEP
Yeah—all six months it lasted.
NEVILLE
Frennie's Aunt Julia tried to evangelize him—
PERI
Maybe I'm not over being married to you, Ti—
WILLIAM
It was all those chicken feathers in his way—
REEP
Think I'll shoot me a Chicken Baby for supper.

PERI

So often, Ti, our words just miss—

TITOMO

I hear everything you say.

REEP

How you doing, ole Chicken Baby? Buck. Buck. I heard you dressed like a chicken and protested the chicken farm.

PERI

Frennie can hear that chicken farm all day—we ought to get her out of there. What's wrong with her husband?

WILLIAM

—especially when it's hot—those chickens make noise— I can smell that chicken farm across town.

REEP

Hey, Chicken Baby—I heard you wear a cross on your back—you walk with your arms tied to the cross beam— you seen her, Neville?

FRENNIE

I thought you were looking for Floral Jean in her Falcon.

PERI

Just like the cat down the road looks at me all day through the kitchen window. We used to stare at people —my friend, Ocholee, and me. We'd pick out an old woman in a drugstore while we drank cokes. Ocholee was good at unraveling people. She got it from her father, who used to leave her on a dirt road outside of Anadarko to see if she could find her way back. I remember when she'd do something he didn't like, and he'd drag her to the car, and soon he'd come back alone. He was in the state hospital for a while. Jail, too, it seems. I think the neighbors complained. Mother said someone ought to. No one had the nerve to do it right out. Finally someone must have called the police.

NEVILLE

Ocholee is gone. The land would get up and walk away, too, if it could.

WILLIAM
> The land's not going anywhere. It's still here under us.

NEVILLE
> Everything has been migrating away from us. We just don't know it yet.

REEP
> Neville still thinks about Ocholee, too.

WILLIAM
> He couldn't get close to her. Her old man put the terror of men into her.

REEP
> I tried after Neville.

TITOMO
> I think one's of Peri's brothers did, too.

NEVILLE
> I called the police. I never told anyone I did.

PERI
> But it didn't keep her from disappearing.

FRENNIE
> Maybe she'll show up.

PERI
> She's gone, Frennie.
>
> I've been wanting to read your mother's recipes, TiTo. I could open those boxes in the shed.

TITOMO
> Why don't you cook?

PERI
> I've already fed your friends. Now they're at the reservoir or the Anadarko Pow Wow. Besides, I work at Neville's Cafe tomorrow.

REEP
> Yahoo! Fritters and homemade pies.

PERI
> I've thought about starting my own cafe—I even thought of a delivery service.

TITOMO
> You've got people enough coming here—

WILLIAM

I'd deliver for you, Peri—

TITOMO

We always got someone here to eat or sleep. Where are your brothers?

REEP

Even those dead folks over there, smelling your cooking, might just get up and walk over here.

FRENNIE

Or one of us might join them.

PERI

There are enough of us over there—Fift, Chune, Aunt Julia. Ocholee is in a graveyard somewhere—now Ti's mother—

TITOMO

I don't want you getting in her boxes yet.

REEP

What could opening a few boxes hurt?

PERI

Your brother doesn't want them. He sent them to you. They're just some of your mother's old things. There might be some recipes.

NEVILLE

Let her open the boxes, man.

TITOMO

I'm ready for another beer.

PERI

I hate for you to drink. You shoot your guns off in the cemetery. Someone will get hurt. You're already doing community service, Ti—it's against the law. What happened to the man I knew?

TITOMO

What happened to the sweet girl I knew?

PERI

Little things don't matter, TiTo, because I have one large complaint—

TITOMO

Which is?

REEP

Man, you shouldn't ask those kind of questions.

TITOMO

You're going to get told anyway, Reep.

PERI

What have we got to do with one another anymore?
When have we been alone?

TITOMO

We've been married twenty years, Peri. I would have
taken you for a ride. I would have gone to the Pow
Wow—

PERI

I just want to stay here with you—

TITOMO

Maybe I'll shoot the sky again. Maybe the stars will
shoot back.

WILLIAM

The reservoir isn't that far. The sheriff hears you, he'll
be back.

TITOMO

(Looking at Peri) You want to be with me—after twenty
years? You got to take me like I am, Peri. I'm getting used
to the rest of my life.

William gets up and goes into the house.

REEP

(Looking at Frennie) Yep—I think I shot an angel in the
cemetery.

NEVILLE

I heard the wings flapping.

FRENNIE

Aunt Julia made angel clothes. She worked her pedal
machine. She made coats with slits to stick their wings
through when they had to fly. Angels have such big feet.
You can hear them in the house at night. The upstairs
floor creaks.

NEVILLE

I think they sleep in pairs.

REEP

> I'm going to get a piece of that gumdrop cake. *(He goes into the house.)*

FRENNIE

> You can lift their angel dresses and see between their legs. They don't need underwear—unless it's winter and they fly over fields covered with ice.

Reep and William come from the house. Reep follows William to his motorcycle in the yard. They look at the motor. William revs it enough to irritate Peri. Frennie holds her ears.

> When Aunt Julia slept, her feet worked the pedal. I could see the sheet move at night. The old pedal of her sewing machine was like an oil pump in the field. Aunt Julia had angels lined up at the door. She kept their clothes in her closets.

PERI

> These old houses don't have closets, Frennie. Aunt Julia kept a wardrobe in the corner. A closet is like a heart. It's what's missing in this house. *(Peri stands on the porch.)*

TITOMO

> You got a heart, Peri. I can feel it beating like those zinnias in the wind—just let me sit with you—

PERI

> —not even owning what is ours. *(Peri walks away.)*

TITOMO

> If you follow her, William—I'm lifting my pistol.

NEVILLE

> He'll shoot more than an angel.

FRENNIE

> It's name was Sulman.

REEP

> *(Returning to the porch)* Whose name?

FRENNIE

> The angel on Aunt Julia's bedroom wall—with sleeves covering his hands.

REEP

> I think Julia ran Frennie through church once too often.

FRENNIE

    I was always afraid of the chickens. They looked like they wore goggles when they flew straight toward us.

REEP

    We should have gone somewhere this weekend.

TITOMO

    I can't sit on a bike for three days anymore.

FRENNIE

    You bikers are the angels of the world.

Section 3

William returns to the porch, where TiToMo sits with Neville and Reep.

WILLIAM

Where's Peri?

TITOMO

I saw her walk to the cemetery—

REEP

She's over there with Frennie and more of the unemployed—all of them—without jobs.

NEVILLE

What's she doing over there?

REEP

Peri's planning to take over your cafe—

NEVILLE

I got my business just the way I want it.

REEP

Hold on to your apron, Neville. She's got her eye on your burners—

WILLIAM

Then you'll know how we feel without anything to stand on. American Gypsies. That's what Indians are. All of us.

TITOMO

We'll be like Reep driving a beer truck.

REEP

It's steady work.

NEVILLE

Maybe Peri's going crazy like Frennie.

TITOMO

Peri knows what she's doing, Neville—she's just crossing the road to see what's there right now—

REEP

She'll scare the sheep. Those gravestones aren't anything but a little flock of lambs—remember?

SECTION 4

Peri and Frennie in the cemetery. Soon, Peri speaks to the people she imagines buried there.

PERI

What's it like down there? Are dreams realized? Are tears wiped away?

Are memories swept up like beer cans after Labor Day?

Is it like drunkenness when we don't remember all we went through to get there? *(She kneels and puts her arm around one of the stones as though it were someone's shoulder.)* Is God there in his majesty or is he really Adelaide, the cat, watching every move I make?

FRENNIE

Are we punished for our sins? Do we get chicken wings?

PERI

Oh, God! Are you real? Are you waiting up like Mother in one of her rages when I came in late from a date with TiTo? Or like his mother, always grumbling about everything? Are you as forgetful as he is of my birthday? *(Pause)* Oh, remember me, God—*(Peri walks to another grave and takes hold of the stone.)* How do we get so careless?

(Peri reads the monument she leans against.) Beth Grant, Beloved Wife of—*(She can't make out the rest of it.)* How many stars for faithfulness? Sometimes I see the children of Galilee around Jesus as he tells his fish stories and always how the biggest one yet is waiting for us on the other side. Never here—though our prairie sky at dusk must be like the desert in Galilee. That's what I always used to think, anyway, when I'd see those pictures in the Bible. Yes, I'd think I've seen that very scene on the road in Oklahoma—*(Peri puts her ear to the monument.)* Tell me, Beth—how did you get marked, *Beloved Wife?*

FRENNIE

I remember when we moved out of the old place into Aunt Julia's house—how our voices echoed off the walls—

PERI

(She leans over a smaller monument and reads the name.) Harriet—Does God look us over like school papers? Does he keep grades? I remember how my mother always went over my school papers. I remember throwing the bad ones in the gutter on the way home from school, and I remember standing beside her as she looked over my good papers and saved them for my father and Frennie and my brothers to see.

You know, these shiny upright stones are just like TV screens.

Do we sit down and talk to one another about what matters?

Does someone take us down the road and let us out to find our way? I remember my friend, Ocholee. Is that death? An old man driving his daughter down the road and letting her out? I bet that's the way it feels. How about it, Edwin? *(She reads another gravestone.)* Was her father really doing her a favor? Did Ocholee know better than us what it's like? Was she more prepared than we are? *(Pause)*

Does God own a cafe? Is there someone to cook for? Does anyone have the old recipe for cottage pudding? Jamaican chicken my great aunt used to make? Rum and diablo sauce? *(Pause)*

I would hate to arrive in heaven and find no tables or kitchen. William says Jesus ate after he went to heaven.

FRENNIE

And here's your grave—Aunt Julia—

PERI

You dragged us out of Indian ways into Christian.

Is there anyone who knows how I feel? I would be happy with TiTo, but he keeps closing the door, catching my fingers sometimes. Do we just put everything in the truck and move on? Turning our keys over to whomever comes along after us?

Are we gypsies on a new migration trail—relocating to the cities, returning to the land—always on our restless travels over highways and roads—never settled?

Don't leave me, TiTo. I'd hate to give it all up yet.

How can we live together and forget how to know one other? TiTo just wants to drink and talk and laugh on the porch with his friends, and when they leave, he's drunk. *(Pause)*

And here are the graves of Fift and Chune, Ti's friends, killed in a bike accident.

I feel so empty, Frennie.

Frennie holds her arm around Peri, comforts her.

You got to go to your own house sometimes, Frennie.

FRENNIE

Sulman, the angel, kept us under his wing.

PERI

(Peri gets up, walks to another stone.) Thurlene—Is the unraveling of this life our punishment? Ocholee—We do good and bad all our lives—and can't help that, either. Or is there neither good or bad, but everything is relative?— as the Indian religion says.

When I am here I want a little cookbook on my grave—

SECTION 5

Peri and Frennie have returned from the cemetery and are in the kitchen. TiToMo, Neville, Reep, and William are on the front porch. It's early evening.

REEP

My stomach's growling louder than William's bike when he turned in the drive.

WILLIAM

Peri's in the kitchen cooking more chicken.

William goes into the house, while the rest of them sit on the porch.

PERI

I can't remember the recipe for the diablo rum sauce for the chicken. I don't have rum, anyway. How's *diablo beer sauce?*—

FRENNIE

The chickens should be covered with angel sauce. If you knew how they suffered—

William picks a gumdrop off Peri's cake. He tastes the chicken and pours more beer in the pan.

PERI

If you pick one more gumdrop off that cake—*(Pause)* The sauce had something in it—some spice I can't remember.

WILLIAM

You got enough red chiles—my mouth's hot as an exhaust pipe.

PERI

I was on the road with you all when my parents and brothers cleaned out Aunt Julia's house. Nobody knows what happened to her recipes. Probably thrown out— with the pictures of angels she had all over the house. My brothers don't have the sense to think what matters to anyone.

Sulman was the angel she kept on her bedroom wall—a sad angel with its hands pulled up in its sleeves—the way we pulled our arms inside our shirts when we were cold. Maybe Frennie's got the picture somewhere. She can pack things away and forget. It's her sort of thing.

TITOMO

(Calls again.) Peri—

PERI

I'm still frying children—chicken—*(To Frennie)* Tell them to get the plates—the napkins, knives, forks, and bowls of food on the table. Stir up that bean salad I got in the fridge, Frennie. The bread's in the oven, darling. Cut the last of that gumdrop cake—whatever is left of it—and have Neville slice the rest of that watermelon William brought.

Soon everyone is in the kitchen.

TITOMO

Where do you want the chicken?

PERI

Anywhere on the table—get that big platter off the top shelf.

TiToMo dishes up the chicken and the men take their food to the porch.

PERI

Ti—I got some relish somewhere in the shed.

TiToMo's already in the yard and doesn't hear Peri. William could tell him Peri asked him to go to the shed, but he doesn't. William goes to the shed but can't find the relish. Soon Peri comes. William tries to embrace her in the shed.

You drink too much over here, Bill, and don't use a brake on yourself. You wait till Ti and I have a hard time, then you jump in like grease.

WILLIAM

I'll take you for a ride.

PERI

I ride with TiTo. Get the relish there on the shelf.

TiToMo and Frennie enter the shed. TiToMo is eating a chicken leg.

TITOMO

What you doing here?

PERI

William's getting the relish.

TITOMO

There's not going to be any chicken left—

PERI

Bill and I been tasting while I cooked. You know I don't eat much after it's done.

Peri hands William the jar of relish.

TITOMO

Don't drink too much more of that beer, Bill—

William takes the relish to the yard. Frennie opens one of TiToMo's mother's boxes before he knows what she's doing. She lifts a Bible from the box. She opens the Bible and finds a letter. She hands it to TiToMo. He drops the chicken leg and wipes his hands on his jeans.

A letter to Mildred Forster, my mother—from Hupata, her father. *(He reads.)* You wanted to go to school. But there was no money. You got married. You left your people, went off to a navy base on the East Coast where you say all the wives are sealed up in their houses.

Remember our tradition. Teach your children. Your mother cries for you. Why did you turn your back on her?

(TiToMo unfolds the pages.) There's other letters—Mildred Forster—my mother—wants something. Money to come home. But there isn't any. She made her decision. She has a husband and two boys to care for. But she misses the land. She wants to be somewhere other than the housing on the base.

TiToMo folds the letters and closes them in the Bible. He sits for awhile in the shed. The others talk and laugh in the yard while they eat.

Open the boxes if you want—*(TiToMo leaves the shed.)*

PERI

    That's why TiTo is afraid of these boxes of his mother's things. They open the old days for him—

FRENNIE

    The smell of yellowed newspaper.

PERI

    Ah! some of her dishes. *(She stops to read bits of the news.) Libya slaps trade ban on Britain. (She continues reading.) A parachuting pig was to be dropped from a plane over the State Fair, but due to public protest, country police arrived with warrants in the names of several committeemen. If the pig were hurt in any way, they were going to get slapped on the spot with a cruelty-to-animals charge. When the plane flew over the fair, it dropped instead a package of freshly ground sausage with a letter saying the pig was now in a form the Society for Prevention to Animals couldn't object to!*

    (Peri is silent a moment as she looks at the old paper. Soon she begins reading more of it—) Mrs. Jones, 56, died of a heart attack Wednesday evening at the home. She was the widow of James P. Jones who died in 1944. (Peri looks at the date of the paper.) Baltimore Banner. 1965. Funeral services for John F. Conklin, 62, an auto salesman for about 40 years, will be held at 10 A.M. Mrs. Bitzer, 93, born in Baltimore County—Surviving are two sons, William J. Bitzer and Woodrow Bitzer, with whom she lived— (Peri scans the paper. She looks quickly at another page of the paper, then tosses it aside and continues to unwrap a few dishes remaining in one of the boxes.) Saucers and bread-and-butter plates. *(She turns to another box.)*

FRENNIE

    An oil lamp like Aunt Julia used to have.

PERI

    Cowboys and Indians that must have been TiTo's and his brother's. Popeye. Baseball cards. A U.S. Navy banner.

FRENNIE

    A compass.

PERI

A picture TiTo drew of his hand. A bride and groom off a wedding cake.

FRENNIE

What a collector—

PERI

(She opens another box and sorts through the things.) Strainers. Muffin tins. Now we're getting to it.

FRENNIE

A six-shooter?

PERI

TiTo's or his brother's, I guess. A recipe box! Recipe books! Jackpot!! His mother's cookbooks!! *(Peri opens one quickly and reads—)* Truss the fowl and cook it in its stock for an hour. While it is cooking, heat the butter—blanch the almonds—shred the onions—slice the raisins, cloves, cinnamon. *(Peri turns the pages of the books.)* Potted carp. Planked mackerel. Sardine toast. Halibut and tomatoes.

FRENNIE

How old are those recipes?

PERI

Chocolate Charlotte. Moon cakes. *(Pauses as she reads further.)* Watermelon rind—that sounds like my recipe. Birthday Delight—Macaroons—Muffins—

Peri keeps reading cookbooks, turning pages of recipes. Frennie grabs the newspapers that blow in the wind.

FRENNIE

The papers are like angels flapping their wings—Peri, what keeps us here? Why don't we blow away like Ocholee?

PERI

It's just the wind that's up, Frennie—making everything flop. *(Peri unwraps a box with an Indian sash in it.)* Look, Frennie, some beading Ti's mother must have done. And here is a rock she kept—she must have taken it from her father's place.

TiToMo returns to the shed. He picks up some of the things Peri has unwrapped and puts them down again. He fingers the six-shooter. The wind picks up a little and blows some papers again. Peri grabs them and weights them down with a corner of a box.

How did your mother get hold of Baltimore papers?

TITOMO

I don't know. Maybe she borrowed a neighbor's paper to wrap her things. Maybe my sister-in-law wrapped them after my mother died.

PERI

And where are the rest of her dishes? I find the cups and saucers, the bowls, but where are the dinner plates? I don't have enough of them when all our friends are here.

Section 6

William, Reep, and Frennie sit on the porch. TiToMo and Neville are in the yard, standing around the motorcycles. It is late evening.

REEP

Look at those gravestones shining like moons—

WILLIAM

(*To Peri as she comes from the kitchen to sit on the porch*) The angels can put their feet on backwards—they get to start again.

PERI

The woman down the road puts out seed for the birds— then watches Adelaide, her cat, stalk them. Yes, she puts out seed—but she loves the destroyer more.

FRENNIE

Aunt Julia held things together for us. How do we find our way back?

PERI

We don't go back, Frennie.

FRENNIE

What do we do?

PERI

We go on. We lost what it was to be Indian. We lost ourselves.

TITOMO

I'm shooting my fear when I lift my pistol.

PERI

What if it shoots back? (*She goes to the yard and stands with TiToMo.*)

TITOMO

Sometimes when we were riding, I'd see bikes pass on the highway—but I didn't know what world they were from.

Sometimes when I try to talk to you, Peri, I hear you close the door.

It was that way when you never wanted to visit my
mother.

PERI

It wasn't an easy ride to see her. She lived on the East
Coast—

TITOMO

I think she would have come back to Oklahoma—if she
thought you wanted her.

PERI

Who else do you want to have with us?

FRENNIE

In the night I can hear the voices of angels.

PERI

In the night I hear the voices of recipes.

SECTION 7

The men are all on the porch. Peri and Frennie are in the kitchen.

REEP

Peri's got a trigger—

TITOMO

She's just touchy because she's getting older.

WILLIAM

She had it her own way, and now she's turned up short.

NEVILLE

She's just mad because everyone talks to the young waitresses now.

TITOMO

I tried to help Peri once and forgot her birthday. She's remembered it ever since. I don't forget anymore, though. Her mama reminds me. I don't have a chance to forget. They're all coming over here next weekend. No—I don't have a chance to do much of anything without Peri telling me about it—

William goes into the kitchen for another beer.

PERI

You've had enough beer, Bill. Slice us a piece of watermelon.

William sits at the table with Peri.

A man is driving down the road behind a farmer with a truckload of pigs when one falls out.

WILLIAM

That's an old one.

PERI

The man stops at a filling station and asks, what do I do with a pig?

WILLIAM

Suppose a pig were following a truckload of farmers— and the pig says, what do I do with a farmer?

FRENNIE

Take him to the chicken farm. Cover him with feathers.

WILLIAM

The shortest distance between two points is a bullet through the air—

REEP

(Entering the kitchen) Buck! Buck!

FRENNIE

Jesus is a chicken herder. Seeker of the lost. We lay our eggs like prayers.

TITOMO

(He comes into the kitchen.) What's up, Peri? You can laugh with Bill but not me?

PERI

It's just me and Bill telling stories, eating watermelon in the kitchen.

WILLIAM

(With his hands on Peri's shoulders) Come on, TiTo—

TITOMO

(Shoves William away from Peri. Angrily—) Don't put your hands on my wife again.

REEP

Everyone—out of here.

Peri stays at the table with her hands over her face. TiToMo touches her head.

PERI

(She pulls away from him.) You leave too!

TiToMo leaves the kitchen. In the yard William grabs TiToMo by the shoulders. TiToMo pulls away. William grabs him again. TiToMo pushes William back.

REEP

Hey—TiTo, break it up! Stop! What else have we got now but friends?

Reep and Neville pull TiToMo away from William. William, out of breath, sits on the porch. TiToMo stands in the yard. Peri comes out of the house and walks across the yard.

WILLIAM

(*Standing, still out of breath, walks toward the cemetery.*) I got to cool off.

TITOMO

Forget it, man—I didn't mean—I get jealous as hell over Peri—you know that—

TiToMo follows Peri to a corner of the yard. Frennie follows TiToMo.

TITOMO

Hey—Tunafish—Wait up. Where you want to go?

PERI

The name's Peri. Somewhere on the prairie where the streetlights don't line up like baby teeth. I want to ride into the stars of the night, TiTo. I want to follow the angels that took off with my Aunt Julia.

TITOMO

Don't know if I got gas that far—

FRENNIE

(*On her hands and knees, pecking in the yard like a hen.*) Cluck. Cluck.

PERI

You're not a chicken, Frennie. Don't cluck. I know you get upset when we fight. The ball lightning struck you in the chicken house. I was there—you didn't turn into a chicken.

FRENNIE

I was born a chicken. Sometimes I think I pecked at the shell.

PERI

No, you didn't.

FRENNIE

The lightning struck me because I was a chicken. I always belonged to the chickens.

PERI

You belong to Jesus, Frennie. Remember what Aunt Julia said?

FRENNIE

> You know the story of Indians when they turn white—
> when they forget their ways, they grow feathers and
> become chickens.

PERI

> I never heard that, Frennie. Just keep Jesus in your head.

TITOMO

> We got stars in Bible school for saying what they wanted.
> Where's my pistol? I want to shoot the stars.

*Reep lifts his pistol and shoots into the air. Neville gets William's
bike to roaring again. He takes off from the yard, rides through the
cemetery. Reep follows. Peri yells after them.*

PERI

> You can't ride through the cemetery—my aunt's over
> there. Fift. Chune. Beth Grant. Edwin. Your friends, TiTo,
> haven't got sense.

*Peri runs after the men. The bikes zoom through the cemetery. Peri
screams at them in fury, gives up, and runs back to the yard. The
bikes continue to tear around the cemetery. Peri covers her ears.*

FRENNIE

> The clouds are the wings of a chicken—It's lightning in
> the chicken house—

*There's wind and lightning. One last shot is heard. Then every-
thing is dark and silent.*

REEP

> What happened? Ti? You're on the ground, man. Get up.

Section 8

Peri and Frennie are on the front porch. Reep rides his bike into the yard. William follows, running. It is dark.

REEP

Peri—

PERI

Where's TiTo?

REEP

TiTo's hurt. We were shooting straight up in the air. TiToMo fell down. There's blood on his head. We can't see in the dark—get a flashlight.

PERI

Use the bike headlight, Reep.

Peri runs behind Reep. There's the sound of Reep's motorcycle riding into the cemetery. Frennie follows them, running. Frennie is crying. Now Peri is screaming.

PERI

(Covering her face in a bright light that appears suddenly in the dark.) There's nothing but the light.

SECTION 9

Peri, Frennie and William are in the kitchen.

WILLIAM

> *(Reading the newspaper)* ANADARKO. *A bullet shot into the air came down with enough velocity to kill a man. Thomas Hampton Forster, age 43, known as TiToMo to his friends, died Labor Day night. His services will be held at the Anadarko Full Gospel Grace Pentecostal Church on Wednesday afternoon. Interment follows in the Anadarko Cemetery.*

FRENNIE

> It was the angels shooting back.

PERI

> It was their own stray bullets, Frennie—turned around and come back down. Without Ti I feel like my bones are gone. Where's my spine?

Frennie holds Peri.

> What happened to us, William? Are we like pigs parachuting over the fairgrounds wrapped in our separate wrappers?

Section 10

TitoMo's funeral in the cemetery. A mix of Indian drumming and Christian hymns. Peri's family, Peri, and TiToMo's friends are grieving. Frennie fans herself in the heat. Peri breaks down in sobs from time to time. William and Frennie try to comfort her.

WILLIAM
> (*Throws a handful of dirt into the grave.*) For Ti—biking in Glory.

PERI
> He's riding with Sulman, Aunt Julia's angel.

NEVILLE
> (*Throws a handful of dirt.*) He's riding with Fift and Chune.

REEP
> (*Throws a handful of dirt.*) Here's to the end of your labor day, man.

NEVILLE
> The whole dark sky's just one reservoir night.

WILLIAM
> You didn't even have to finish your community service.

NEVILLE
> Now you can shoot anywhere, Ti, and not get arrested.

PERI
> Find Ocholee, my friend, for me, TiTo.

NEVILLE
> (*Throws dirt into the grave.*) You're out there in cool space, TiToMo—find Ocholee for me, too.

REEP
> Your grave is catercorner to your house.

NEVILLE
> Peri's keeping you close to home.

FRENNIE
> The wind is a biker in the trees.

PERI

Ti is with his parents now.

FRENNIE

Ti is with Aunt Julia now.

REEP

(Throws a handful of dirt.) Ti's got his freedom.

WILLIAM

Just what he was afraid of.

PERI

Here's some of your mother's stuff, Ti. I got them from her boxes. I toss them into your grave. Here's the base-ball cards. A U.S. Navy banner. A compass. Six-shooter. Here's the past for you. Tell her I'm keeping the recipes.

FRENNIE

Maybe Ti was trying to shoot an angel out of the sky for you, Peri.

PERI

I think he was shooting the angel away—

Section 11

Neville, Reep, and Peri are at Neville's Cafe. Neville is wiping the plastic covers of menus. Peri is in the kitchen, making a racket with the pans while Neville and Reep talk.

NEVILLE

What're you doing in there, Peri?

PERI

(From the kitchen) Trying to serve something other than grease.

NEVILLE

This is my cafe. You don't have Ti behind you anymore.

Peri walks into the cafe, throws the menus into the air. They hit the floor with a clunk. Peri returns to the kitchen. The men look at the menus on the floor. Neville picks them up, starts wiping them again.

REEP

Stand back from ole *Peril*.

NEVILLE

We were all shooting in the air.

REEP

You think one of us killed him?

NEVILLE

Any of our bullets could have come back down and struck Ti. There's no way to know.

More banging in the kitchen.

REEP

His own bullet hit him.

PERI

(Coming from the kitchen again.) I can't stay here, Neville. I got to Powwow someplace else.

REEP

I was getting ready to order some of your turnips and ham.

PERI

Maybe Neville will cook you some of his reservoir fish.

Peri leaves the cafe.

SECTION 12

Peri, Frennie, and William are in the cemetery.

PERI

We could make Aunt Julia's house a boarding house—
a bed-and-breakfast.

WILLIAM

I thought you still worked at Neville's.

PERI

I walked out of his place—

WILLIAM

He thinks you're coming back—

FRENNIE

The interstate bypasses Anadarko.

PERI

Not by much—

FRENNIE

Who would come?

PERI

We can take in angels when they come to the earth.

WILLIAM

I'd stay at your place, Peri. I was your first—

PERI

TiTo is still my life, William. You're happiest when you
reach for someone you can't have. You've got a gypsy
heart.

FRENNIE

(Frowning at him) We're at TiTo's grave, William—

PERI

(Speaking to TiToMo's grave) Take me for a ride, TiTo. I
want to lose ten years. When we traveled, our hands
were full of wings.

There's more heat lightning in the sky.

The stars were the eyeballs of the night. I want to mount
the white saddle of the half-moon. I hear my name from

the sky. A voice says, *come,* Peri Aden Forster, widow of
Thomas TiToMo Forster, niece of Julia Halex, friend of
Sulman, the bedroom angel, daughter of Mark and Mary
Aden, sister of Frennie and three brothers, daughter-in-
law of Hamp and Mildred Forster—

FRENNIE

I want to ride too—*(She also speaks to TiToMo at his grave.)*
Remember how you'd come and get us in school, TiTo?
We'd fly over the roads. Remember how I wanted to ride
with Reep? Remember how I fought with Floral Jean
over him?

WILLIAM

Neville wouldn't ride with anyone if Ocholee wouldn't
ride with him.

PERI

We have to go on now, Frennie—by ourselves.

FRENNIE

You always went first, Peri. I followed. Take me where
you go. The world is full of lightning. We have to be careful where we step. It's why the chickens were struck with
lightning—because they were afraid. It's why the little
ball of lightning jumped at me. But if we stand still, the
lightning won't know we're afraid.

WILLIAM

Remember in church when the Holy Ghost fell? You and
Ocholee chicken-walked until Aunt Julia would call you
down.

FRENNIE

That's why we're gypsies. That's why we lost our land.
So we won't be stuck here. So we can be ready to leave
this earth.

PERI

I saw a light in the cemetery the night TiTo was killed.

FRENNIE

Peri's in a chicken funk over Ti.

PERI

Sometimes something gets into your head and you can't

get it out. It was Labor Day. Then TiTo was dead. What happened? We are here. We are there. It's as fast as that and just as lasting.

FRENNIE

In church I always carried the candle snuffer. I was the one who put out the light.

WILLIAM

It's our pain that's the light, Peri. We can see inside ourselves when we hurt. All the stubbornness and determination. All the selfishness.

FRENNIE

I think the chickens come for you, Peri, when you die.

PERI

I think my friend, Ocholee, will come for me. All I can think of is the recipe for diablo sauce I was looking for—that's just what Ocholee would hand me from the other world.

SECTION 13

Frennie and Reep on the road to the chicken farm. Frennie is dressed in chicken feathers. She wears a cross on her back. Frennie walks down the dirt road holding a sign—They die so we can live.

FRENNIE

It's this heat that makes them suffer—They just can't think in the heat—

REEP

(Reep approaches on his bike. Slows.) I heard you were out here, Frennie.

FRENNIE

What are you bothering me for? You left me once. You're still after Floral Jean.

REEP

Buck. Buck.

FRENNIE

You watch out for chickens. They been heated up so long they're mean.

Reep follows her on the road, gunning his motorcycle. Frennie turns and hits him with her sign and leaves him fallen from his bike on the road.

SECTION 14

William, Peri and Frennie are in the shed.

WILLIAM

> What do you want for your birthday, Peri?

PERI

> I want TiTo.

WILLIAM

> You're too close to the cemetery, Peri. We always stay too close to what we shouldn't—

PERI

> Frennie's going to stay with me awhile. It would be like we were at Aunt Julia's again—

FRENNIE

> I thought we couldn't go back.

PERI

> We're moving on—wherever it takes us.

WILLIAM

> You're taking Frennie without much thought for her. What does Frennie's husband say about this?

FRENNIE

> I want to be at the American Gypsy Cafe—Chicken Baby's Boarding House—

WILLIAM

> Nobody would drive down here to the end of the road.

FRENNIE

> There are travelers all over the back roads of America, William—There are maps of the bed-and-breakfasts— There are maps for bikers—

PERI

> I'm going to bake a white cake for my birthday and pile it with icing until you think it's chicken feathers, Frennie. I'm going to find the plastic bride and groom in TiTo's mother's boxes—I'm marrying the rest of my life.

FRENNIE

Dad said you get some widow's benefits, Peri. You can make the house payments—you can stay here. You spent years on the road with TiTo—always moving away from me—everything changes except at Aunt Julia's. She was good, Peri. How did she stay so good?

PERI

It would kill me to be that good.

FRENNIE

She was missing part of herself. The bad part.

PERI

She was torn out somewhere—something left a hole.

FRENNIE

You know the moon always wanted to get back to the earth. I see it sometimes and know it does. No, the moon is a chicken head. Buck. Buck. I hear it up there in the sky.

WILLIAM

You can see the moon sometimes in the day. Stranded with a rod or something missing. A loose moon rolling down a dirt road.

PERI

(Peri holds Frennie.) Sometimes I saw Aunt Julia standing at the window—when we played in the cemetery— when we'd come down the road to her house. There at the window—I'd see her face.

FRENNIE

Sometimes a chicken gets into your head like a stray bullet.

What happened to the chicken coop, Peri?

PERI

Aunt Julia tore it down—after you kept talking about the lightning.

FRENNIE

Aunt Julia said she had Jesus in her heart. I think he got in with his pistol and shot the hell out of there—then he moved in with his gear.

PERI

I think the chickens peck the barnyard as if they were angels looking for a place to land. They bump into one another. They can't see out the front of their heads. They can't ask for help—their beaks don't form words we understand—and when we speak they can't hear because their ears are tucked inside their feathers as if in a biker's cap—their eyes are the goggles we should dread.

Jump Kiss

"Take your ice-chopper
break up that block—"

CITY COUNCIL (REPHRASED) TO THE AUTHOR,
AFTER A FINE FOR SHOVELING TOO NARROW A PATH.

PLATE I

My Ears Tuned to the Spirit Realm
Characters
Glow-ree
Photo
When Clouds Were Suds
My Composition on Rocks
Galoshes
Scars
An Explanation Tale
Downwind, Father
Cold

PLATE II

Moving the Grandparents from the Farm
Fragment
Setting
Birdlime
A Greater Oven
Head Binding
The Cherokee Strawberry Legend
Street Crud

PLATE III

Northwest Link Flight #3220, Minneapolis-Lincoln
The Stockyards
Fragment

Credo
Fragment
Fragment
Fragment

PLATE IV

Etiology
Lung
A Preliminary Moses
Jump Kiss
Vacation Bible School

PLATE V

Fragment
Too Bad He Didn't Know What He Had
Divorce
Miscarriage
Fragment
The Clearing

PLATE VI

A Place between Two Trees
Deathbed
Tattoo
Fragment

PLATE VII

The Piece of Red Licorice
Rock Concert
Their Graves
Dancing Man
There Has To Be Something about Reconciliation
Fragment
Fragment
My Ears Tuned to the Spirit Realm

I melt the frost flowers at the kitchen window
with my breath.

MANFRED KARGE, MAN TO MAN

WORKING NOTES

Jump Kiss rides upon plates like the earth's crust. I suppose the seven movable plates could be read in a different order. *Jump Kiss* is a search for definition of self, fragmented by the act of memory, buckling events, pushing one plate under another. Disordering the landscape in other words.

Acrylic and mixed-media. A title I saw on a painting. I want to do that with writing. A new *genre-tive* blend of the fictive and nonfictive. Maybe it could be called *epi-drama.* Or *para-drama.* Even the *sur-dramatic voice.* Because I want to experiment with form. Maybe the pieces could be called *broken drama* or *voice fragments.* Taking place in the dark of the head. Maybe some minimal movement of the eyes across the page. The way light fluctuates on a panel during recording.

You know, maybe if a piece didn't have action—if voice was all it had—

I wrote the play as a diary or journal piece to enclose different voices and genres—some of the pieces are narrative (exposition) for the purpose of story. Other pieces are more poetic or experimental.

Jump Kiss is an explanation ceremony. A recovery of events and experiences and relationships for the purpose of understanding what has passed.

PLATE I

MY EARS TUNED TO THE SPIRIT REALM

One night Grandmother Spider crept on the binding of
my book, yet my hand reached instinctively and sput
out the life.

CHARACTERS

There are no voices yet. But the four of us at the kitchen table each facing a different direction. Father North. Mother South. Brother East. Sister West. Four people at the four corners of the earth.

Without music. Without books.
Without spirit though we went to church.

We had meat my father brought home from the stockyards
where he worked.
And there was anger.
And a repression of it.
You could see the residue when you looked.
The rings of water on the table when you lifted the glasses.

And impatience.

Everything stark, white, decent.
Except for the flashes of anger and the lack of meaning.

We were middle-of-the-road
don't-rock-the-boat kind of people.

A wrapped environment. The sculptor, Christo, who wrapped the coast of Australia in canvas, or a part of the coast, in something like a tepee hide. The whole coast would have been inconceivable.

And our house was under some sort of wrapping.
We were driven far into ourselves on our opposite corners,
the primitive, cold mornings
when we got out of bed in the cave
wrapped in animal robes. Grunting.
Our nightmares still hanging on the wall,
most of them upside down.

And the hunger for something you could hold in your hand.

Cooking was my mother's small eruption
the volcanic mountain on the coast
the explosion of gas into flame
the hopping of the dress as her body whipped
potatoes.

We were beat if we got sick. And she hated messes. She
wanted the sterility of the afterlife while we yet lived.
She was always reaching through the years pulling
death over her lap like an afghan.

I didn't have. I wasn't. I couldn't.

I have to realize what they did. He came from
Arkansas to the stockyards in Kansas City. She came
from the farm with a cedar chest and orange blossoms.
When they married she already faced south.
He was headed north.

No one helped or gave him anything.
She had intelligence and didn't know what to do with it.
She kept us to ourselves.
The frustration of sheets that sailed the clothesline like
ghost ships with land always out of reach.

She found what all sailors know.
The slow suffocating movement of life across the vast
sea of her face.

But where does this happiness come from?
Because of the hints of life I saw on the white
iceberg of the wall?
Because of Christ himself?

GLOW-REE

What does God require?

That we live righteously before Him.

Can we do that?

No.

Then what hope is there?

Christ died for us.
Inside Him, there's a cave
where light doesn't shine us up like pure white teeth.

PHOTO

There was always a pine tree pointing up. Something
that doesn't like to bow. Isn't there something in us
that moves against it? Isn't that the shape of prayer?

I look at the picture of me and my father. His eyes so
dark they snapped. I remember him in the dark when
I pet my cat and her fur sparks the cold.

He and I stood together in the yard under the pointing
top of the pine. It must have been a joy to him to take
us out on Sunday. He would rather have slept or read
the newspaper. No, he would rather have listened to
the ball game, but she had him by the neck. Alone with
us all week, she made him serve his time on Sunday.
So he's holding me there in the yard. Our shadow
reaching the pine. The trunk reaching the limbs.
The limbs touching the sky.

I'm in a dress with puffed sleeves. How I twinkled
on the lawn like a July sparkler. No, an overdressed
grape. Behind us, the dark, open hole of the door. The
rickrack of the basement stairs. Down there he show-
ered and I sat on the stairs watching. The first smell
of soap against his skin when he came home from
the stockyards. Why did she let me watch him who
wouldn't let me do anything? His dark, hairy body,
the soap on his shoulders like crumbs of rock candy.

He wishes he'd been a vacuum cleaner salesman. Or a
shipper of kangaroos to distant parts, returning home
only once every one hundred years. I would still be
the same sugar baby. The piece of fudge for him.

WHEN CLOUDS WERE SUDS

Poles for the clothesline were the first things pounded
in the yard when we moved. Clothesline stretched
between the poles was our umbilical cord. Rows of
flowers up the backyards vanished into the universe
at the top of the block. She washed and hung out
clothes until the clouds were suds from her white
naptha soap. We were early astronauts tied together
under the sky. Her fingers fumbling to unpin
my hands.

MY COMPOSITION ON ROCKS

I have rocks from every place I've been. One rock is a
turquoise heart. I think of it placed in the crate of my
ribs. Another is a chicken gizzard wrapped in waxed
paper. I have a rock that was the tongue of a creek in
Santa Fe. Not in the town but in the hills. The water
spoke to me that warm day. I hear rocks. They sing
hymns. "Blessed Be the Rock of my Salvation." My
composition about rocks is a voice to God. I have a
rock like the rock Moses smote for water in the wilderness. I have a rock that could be a cooking stone you
heat in a fire and drop in the pot. Rocks are very
important minerals. Some of them are man-made.
I have a brick from a burned church in Kentucky. I
have another brick printed *Coffeyville.* I got it from a
brick street in Kansas when no one was looking. This
is my piece called *My Rock Collection.* It is a composition describing the rocks in my collection. One rock
looks like a tenderloin with a strip of fat still on it. My
father worked for the stockyards, you know. I found
the rock in Arizona along a road. *Who is a Rock save our
God?* There are greater and lesser rocks. I have a rock
with a round fossil in it. Another is the shape of the
butte where Texas drops into New Mexico on
Interstate 44. Some rocks are sandstone, quartz,
granite. The quartz rock sparkles with silver fillings.
One rock is square like a kitchen table covered with
an oilcloth. Another rock has the gooseflesh of a swimming cap. I have a volcanic rock. A lily-pad rock like
the lake in Arkansas where we fished. Then a rock that
feels like pumice, but I don't know what it is.

GALOSHES

Later, his hands were lily pads on my chest. I wanted
his whole body over me. Then I remember a children's
book I had, *Jeremy Fisher*. He was a frog who lived on a
lily pad. Oh, what happened to him? He jumped in the
water in his galoshes. I think a trout ate him but spit
him out because of the taste of rubber. Isn't that the
way with love? Something like the taste of galoshes?

SCARS

The burn opened the skin on my legs
so the air could get in.
I know bones need air.
That was it, wasn't it? Why it happened.
So the bones could breathe.

When I knelt down on the fire
under the open grate of the floor furnace
in the old grocer's.
There must have been the sound of crickets.
Melting galoshes and snowsuit.
The crunching of all their bamboo cages.

Cleft of the Rock.
Scar like the skin of a swimming cap.
Lily pad.

Maybe I was running from the greater hurt.
Her fingernails filed to short points.
Her knobs and fine tuners.
The wire rack.

My scars are the frost on windowpanes in winter.
My scars are the crinkled face of the moon.

It was an accident.
Burning my legs.
But nothing's an accident.
Maybe I wanted to fall into the yellow flames
like a leaf.

AN EXPLANATION TALE

My father didn't go to WWII because he worked for
the stockyards. He was exempt because he was a food
producer. Instead, his line of prisoners marched up the
kill chute. Inside, they were strip-searched. He brought
home the liver and rump roasts in white wrappers.

Sometimes, at the kitchen table, I saw the four of
us waiting our turn. The feedlot and the cross were
connected. God the lead goat and Christ the lamb
of sacrifice.

I hear Father God, the rungs of His chair scraping the
floor. The smell of the cedar box I bought on a trip
to see Grandmother Hall. The Indian one.

The cedar box small enough for a rock. Like our Christ.
His flesh poked with nails, because I was mean to my
brother. I stole his nickel.

I wonder if I ever loved them. I can stand at their grave
and cry. But what do I feel? Does it matter? The scratch
of his bristly face. The blast of his car out the drive.

DOWNWIND, FATHER

I walked down the hall, a pull toy scraping the shore.
I opened the door into their room and found what all
sailors know. *Go back. Get in bed.* The door slammed
like heavy waves up and down the corridor of the sea.

COLD

Just now the cold is rising.

The snow outside is a swimming cap
falling across the yards.
You remember those rubber caps
pitted as gooseflesh
the girls had to push their hair up under?

Father. Mother. Brother. Sister.
Stirring in the house.
No.
The brother in his galoshes in the yard.

Frost crawling up the windows like old leaf-veins.

Inside the elements of the kitchen
air
earth
fire
water

Now there was snow.

PLATE II

MOVING THE GRANDPARENTS
FROM THE FARM

It takes all day to loosen the soil. The heavy boxes
against the walls of the farmhouse. The table, beds,
chairs tied down.

The heat breaks in the night. On our mattresses, we
don't die enough but hold our bones with wrench and
pliers. Next morning the circus clouds toss over us.

My father backs the station wagon to the house. My
mother takes more boxes to the car. Dishes my grandmother doesn't want broken. Rain falling behind our
ears, running down our noses.

All summer the heat snapped us like a fire. No, this
rain we haven't had waits until moving day.

She takes the picture off the wall. Van Gogh's
sunflowers with petals like hangnails of a cherub.
A flock of sunflowers hanging over a vase with
green stalks like goosenecks.

In the house my grandmother would have left her
teapot on the stove. Ah! Now she finds the cat, last
thing dragged to the car.

In the yard my father hooks the station wagon to the
house. We get in the car, drag the house from its foundation, bugs running, pipes dangling behind, like roots
of an old tree.

A spent hurricane must be making its way north.
We drive down the farm road to the small town.
Lamp shades rocking in the back of the station wagon.
Everything coming to bare ground, pulling a sled over
snow and hitting a shoveled walk and pulling anyway.

I hear the low, wild whine of the car and house as we hump the farm road. Sunflowers bending in the ditches. The strokes of their stalks. Streams of them like rickrack I sewed on a blouse in home ec.

In town they find a vacant lot for the house. We're clowns coming out of a midget car, carrying boxes of dishes. Moving chairs back into their place, hanging the blessed sunflowers. Over the sky the geese fly south again under broken clouds. Five trips to the hardware to hook up everything again. Then night and the first lights bloom on a string. The small place all full of its own goosey light.

FRAGMENT

I have a rock that looks like a piece of candy.
When I hold it
I see my grandparents flapping their wings.
I see them as children knocking on hereafter's door
with their sacks.

SETTING

All day we share the house.
The low sun is a car
with one headlight turning in the drive.

In places the floor is covered with pine needles.
There are flattened pinecones on the rug
when horses stampede the house.

The trees are fishnets
where a man could lose his catch.

I hear the wind when we travel too long.
A ghost who haunts the search.

I look for the dark to hide us
taking potshots at the road signs
and the one light of the sun.

BIRDLIME

She was vacuuming the bird room.
I didn't know what to do other than be in the way.
I tripped over the ottoman and cried.
I remember her anger I was hurt.
It was probably the same day I wanted to go outside
and she said it was too cold
but I kept wanting to go out.
Finally she put on my snowsuit
and when I got outside it was too cold.
I wanted back in.
I remember she ripped the snowsuit off.
I remember the chores she didn't want to do,
complaining until the sun was back from South
America.
Then she walked to the garden with the zinnia seeds,
a pink scarf on her head,
a sack of birdlime in her hand.

A GREATER OVEN

The furnace is the greater oven. The stove, the lesser.
The other forces are gravity and electromagnetism.
Just as there were four of us.
Mother. Father. Sister. Brother. The four-ces
that held our world together.

My mother stood at the stove, whipping mashed potatoes. Her dress and apron jiggling and my father saying,
OOOOOO-eeee!

Her oven face heated up then. In that narrow kitchen.
That dinghy afloat on a farm pond.

The oven blast of her slap.

It was a metal box. A death camp.

The whole stove white as a swimming cap.

HEAD BINDING

Sometimes she'd open her hand
and I'd see a blue light.

Come in here, she said,
and put a tight swimming cap on my head.

If I touched her I got frostbite.

THE CHEROKEE STRAWBERRY LEGEND

The first man and woman lived in harmony for a time. Then they began to quarrel. At last the woman left and started off to the Sun Land in the East. The man followed, but the woman kept steadily ahead and never looked back.

The sun took pity on the man and asked him, *Are you still angry with the woman?*

He said, *No.*

Would you like to have her back again?

He answered, *Yes.*

The sun caused many things to spring up in the woman's path. A patch of huckleberries. A clump of blackberries. But the woman passed them by. She kept steadily on until she came to some large, ripe strawberries. The woman stopped to gather a few to eat, and as she picked them, the memory of her husband came back. She sat down, but the longer she waited, the stronger the desire for her husband became. At last she gathered a bunch of the red berries and started back along the path to give them to him.

STREET CRUD

You know what's strange? I didn't miss him. I was married nearly twenty years, and then it was over. You'd think you'd feel a person's absence after all those years.

It's harder now. He used to make money and I had a house. Now I rent a place and park my car in a garage down the alley because the car won't fit into mine. I have to stop my car and back into the garage, pulling forward again, then back, slowly into the opening. The fence and bushes are right on the alley, and I can't get the big car into the garage. Then I squeeze between the wall and the car, getting street crud on my coat and purse. I pull down the wooden door, walk up the alley to my house. It's always snowy. Always below freezing. When I was married, I only had to turn into the drive and push my garage-door opener. I didn't even have to feel the winter air on my face and legs. Why am I happier now?

Sometimes when I lift the door, the snow falls into the coat sleeve of my raised arm.

I had a house once.
With Indian legends running up the stairs.

PLATE III

NORTHWEST LINK FLIGHT #3220, MINNEAPOLIS-LINCOLN

The propellers twirl like a child's two hands
throwing fits.
Tell me why I put my life in a windup toy.
The vibration jump kissing my legs.
The whole plane tipping on its toes,
running toward the sky with a roar.

Then down there in the toy box,
a river,
some trees still without leaves
though I look every day.

Above the air the propellers are nearly invisible.
Just a gray image,
a funnel cloud with a tiny, jagged lightning streak
of reflected light.
And an arch something like a jump rope over heaven.

Up here I can see beyond what is visible.
I can rock in a hammock
tied to the horns of the moon.

I can think of someplace I almost was
but got thrown back from,
and fell like an angel from heaven
in the small child of the plane,
landing then throwing its tantrum
in the backwards roar of the engine.

THE STOCKYARDS

Every morning the cows went up the chute to the kill. The lead goat got through all right, but the others— ping. That silver nail. Right through the brain. They were sliced as if a loaf of bread on legs. Wowie. The smell of death falling back on them. They knew it was coming. They knew. And maybe they bucked a little, but the line drew them forward. Just like in the movies where the cowboy is strapped to the sawmill belt and is fast moving toward the saw.

I dreamed once my father took us to the barbershop to cut off our heads. He held my brother on his knee. I woke before they got to me. But the fear—you know, when you wake still in the dream and your flesh is crawling with chills—those chemicals released when you dream so you can't move. So you don't take the room with you while your father and the barber slit your brother's throat with a knife—and now your father's looking at you—

The wide eyes and nostrils of the cows as they smelled death—

It was later, though, I had to kill myself before I could go on to life.

A ritual I had to do.

FRAGMENT

I never hired her, but she was there as Mother. Her beak
and feathers. Her house shoes stretched over her claws.
She probably thought she hadn't hired me. We two
snagged ourselves on the same robe. Making beds, turning mattresses, asking why there were no bird-socks.

CREDO

I believe in the stockyards and the cows that suffer death.

On the third day they ascend into heaven.

They come again in glory to judge the living and the dead, and their kingdom shall have no end.

FRAGMENT

See Christ going up the ramp. To the cross. So God
His Father can look down and shoot the silver nail into
His head and say hey, you dead and in that death sin's
punished and then He gets zipped up in a cave and
comes alive and jump kisses heaven. On Sunday
mornings, the arms raised, the tongues stuttering,
the glory, the power is all yours, Christ.

FRAGMENT

I needed it so. Forgiveness.

But you know Christ doesn't care who you are or what you've done. He opens you like a pear. Takes His pearing knife right down to the core. It doesn't hurt. Does a pear feel pain? Have you ever heard one cry out as you bit into it?

FRAGMENT

The stockyards where my father worked had wooden
floors. The old buildings got too expensive to repair.
Then shipping the cattle to the city got expensive.
The railroads and cattle trucks, you know,
and the old plant was razed.

Now the cattle are born, fed, killed, and processed
in the same place.
Just drive out across the plains.
You'll know where they are.

PLATE IV

ETIOLOGY

I guess *jump kiss* is like a jump shot. My son always liked basketball. I got the idea on a link flight. The vibrations of the small plane jumped my legs. Sensual in a way. But definitely jarring the way flight usually felt. I wanted to try something out of reach. The height of a hoop. I guess.

The whole tree turning a leaf.

With the asking of a blessing of mercy and grace from the old structure for the new.

LUNG

His lung collapsed a day ago. A doctor inserted a tube, had to try several times to get it in the soft part of the chest, nearly under the arm, close to the nipple. Now he can't breathe again.

Hurry. The car followed the dark curve of the hill.

Back to the emergency room where we had been for stitches and X rays from ball games and Boy Scouts. Now his lung collapsed a second time. He's seventeen, in the middle of his senior year, a basketball player.

Only not the first doctor anymore. Now the surgeon. He would insert a tube into the boy's lung. He would do it only once, he saw the three holes he already had. We would go to the waiting room. I could see his dread as we left. After 3:00 in the morning now and he would suffer again, no matter how swiftly and with what ease it was done.

The surgeon came to us when he finished. He sat on the edge of the table and talked to us with calmness. He had X rayed the lungs. There were several holes in the upper right corner. It would take surgery to correct.

We looked at him. What caused it?

Inheritance or pushing himself. Who knows? Maybe he hadn't known when to stop. Maybe we hadn't known when to stop him.

The holes would be stapled and he should be good as new. *Count yourselves fortunate.* It's something he could fix.

You have to have surgery. The doctor had already explained it. His eyes were red from the insertion of the tube, which was left in this time and attached to some sort of pump on a cart beside him.

I thought of the babies somewhere just born. Cozy in their little beds. His sister was still in her bed at home. We had not wakened her when he left. But the cats knew.

Don't worry. Two orderlies rolled the boy and the cart to the elevator and up to a room. We followed. The anesthesiologist would be in in the morning to tell him the procedure for the surgery. The orderlies had seen a lot of these. They put him in bed and said we could leave. No, we would not. I stayed on the empty bed in the room. His father sat in the chair. Nothing moved and we were suspended until dawn. No breakfast. The nurses took blood, adjusted the bottles on the end of the tube coming out his lung. I sat up groggy. The light came in the window like a saw.

Another blood test. An hour passed. The anesthesiologist appeared and arrogantly told us he would administer the medication and be with him all the time. We were not comforted. After the holes were stapled, the lining of the lung would be rubbed until, irritated, it secreted something that would make the lung stick to the lining and not ever collapse again. His incision would be stitched, and he could go home in a week.

We rode the elevator down with him and got off but could go no farther. I wanted to touch his head—say something, but I would not bawl in front of him when he had surgery before him.

His father and I went to the waiting room, where we passed several hours with people from the church and some of the basketball mothers who came.

I thought of the incision in his chest. Where would it be? How long?

The doctor called when the surgery was over. The boy was in the recovery room, and when he woke, he would be taken upstairs to intensive care. We could go up when we wanted.

We waited another hour or two, standing in the hall, looking at every cart off the elevator. Then it was him. Some other people from church were with us then—

Awake and in pain, *It's over,* I said when his gurney was beside us.

It's over, he repeated what I said, whispering as though it was not. This child delivered to us again, bundled in bandages and pain.

A PRELIMINARY MOSES

I think of my son on the table during surgery.
His lung collapsed as though it were a crumpled
wrapper
in a paper bag.
Over him my father in the garage
rubs water on an inner tube
to find the fizzz where air leaked.
I sit in the waiting room
sewing a rip in the knee of his jeans.
The doctors pull out his lung.
Unfold the holes
and my father glues on a piece of rubber.
Afterwards the door breaks open with his gurney
like my father rolling a tire.
Place a hand anywhere and there is pain.
Every breath stretches the wound.
Swelling flesh pulls at the stitches.
I would have bit threads loose with my teeth.
The respirator rattles.
The suction pump with tubes from his lungs
churns the river to blood.
Later he can lift his arm
to walk his fingers up the wall.
Remembers when he could throw a ball
before the lung collapsed
and a scar like the Red Sea closed his chest.

JUMP KISS

You are my shield and high motion.
My toe stub.
My roster.
My jump kiss.
My favorite one.

VACATION BIBLE SCHOOL

There was nothing but voices until our teacher clapped
her hands. Another girl and I were a large rock. *A boul-
der,* the teacher told us. The space between us was the
cleft in the rock where she stood, Moses when God
passed.

Our vacation Bible school teacher believed in learning
through dramatic tableau.

We were the plagues in Egypt.
We wore red cloaks when the river turned to blood.
We were frogs.
We were locusts.
We were lice.
Then followed pestilence.

When a backdrop fell after the Exodus
we headed into the wilderness with a *jump start.*

PLATE V

FRAGMENT

Back in the house again
humm humm the chores
downstairs something rumbles
some old housewife still at her stove
some basement shower running
some *boogaloo*
out across the yards
the grass under snow.

I have a rock that looks like a strawberry.

I would hold you in my arms
I would rock you all right
I would plug in the rumbling vacuum cleaner
with its steady light unbroken on the rug.

I climb the electric cord into the wall.

TOO BAD HE DIDN'T KNOW WHAT HE HAD

See them on the wedding cake wrapped young and
awkward.
Not having a clue what they were about.
His suit too large.
His dear pregnant bride.
Backing out from it now.
The long line of grandparents father mother brother
husband children grandchildren holding her, saying
come-on-now-it-won't-hurt-much.

DIVORCE

I don't know why I can't get over him. It's been more than five years now since we've been divorced and I won't even think about him for weeks and then his mother calls and says what a hard time he's having and I think, *so what*. Maybe he deserves it, and I'm mad because I'm tired just coming in off the road and she digs up all that anger again. The remembrance of how he bragged around the office how easy he got off. Everyone told me. He hid the money, kept the house. That man has the house! The savings. And he buys this ring for a woman in the office fifteen years younger than him, and soon they're married and she and her son move in the house. My children are out, and now we have to make it on our own. He's always telling us what we can do without. He's lost every job since I can remember. The first time he lost his job, we were married only a year and a half and he decided to go back to school. His mother paid for it, of course. Usually when I had dinner on the table, she'd call and they'd yell across the miles at each other and I'd be sitting there with the kids eating my asparagus wondering what marriage was about. Well, we're divorced now and I talk to him and get just as mad as if we were still married. Only now the loneliness isn't as bad as it was when I was married. Then it was tough. Now I'm just poor and angry and tired all the time from my traveling job. But I'm on my own.

Now of course we're not getting into what was wrong with me. I'm not telling why I was unappealing. Why I couldn't be loved or even matter enough to bring him home from work instead of drinking with the boys. Not that I cared, finally. Sometimes I wished he wouldn't come home at all. But he did, and after twenty years, I thought this could go on another twenty. I had an affair, I did, and this dude taped us making love and sent it to my husband on my birthday. Just three weeks before the divorce was final, and my husband said if I asked for anything he'd play the tape for the children and the judge, and I wouldn't get anything. I should be satisfied with the alimony he was going to give me. But he soon tired of sending a check every month and finally none came. I was on my tail for awhile. But the worst of it, I will tell you. I was pregnant by this man, but I miscarried after the second month. I was pregnant and still lived in my husband's house before the divorce. We hadn't slept in the same room for a long time, but I should have been roasted on a spit. I should have burned at the stake. But I feel like I'm forgiven. I feel free of it all.

MISCARRIAGE

I got back to the house about 3:00. I was bleeding then.
And the smell. I thought of rusted iron. Not clean. And
I'd been at school with children. But it waited until I
got back. I went in to the bathroom and felt the clump
pass quickly. I flushed the toilet. It was all red.

I lay on the bed. My kids came in from school. My son
had a basketball game that night. I felt blood running
from me. I changed the pad several times. I also called
the doctor, but he was gone so I left a message.

I don't remember if I went downstairs and cooked dinner that night. I suppose I did. It's what I did every
evening. But I know there was a basketball game I
went to that night. My son played. Afterwards there
was a party for one of the mothers. Other parents were
in the room. I went in the bathroom now and then.

There was a strange relief it was over and at the same
time a sadness.

The doctor called the next day and wondered what
happened to me. He said he'd called several of the
hospitals. I asked if people went there after a miscarriage. He said often yes, because of the bleeding. Well,
I'd already slowed down. I didn't want to go. He
asked me to come in the next week.

And the father. I called him that evening.

FRAGMENT

Sometimes when I bring a new rock home, the others won't talk to it for awhile.

THE CLEARING

The hissing slips from my dreams again.
I cover my mouth, struggle to wake.
Once, a husband pulled me into the clearing.
I tasted bean bread, Indian meat pie, dried corn
pudding.

Now I grope in the woods again
pulling woven baskets and a pine-needle mattress—
My tongue flickers like lightning.
My heart, coiling, waits to strike.

PLATE VI

A PLACE BETWEEN TWO TREES

SISTER

> When she put dinner on the table, I thought it was a
> photo on my plate. An old photo of a man with a hat
> pushed back on his head, in overalls and a white shirt
> and tie, as if a foreman inspecting the trees, come to
> see if they were doing their job of shading.

BROTHER

> Do you know why he went there?

SISTER

> I think it was to judge the trees.
> You know the story of when the trees were supposed
> to stay awake, but they slept—except for the pines. It's
> the pine that gets to keep its covering all winter. The
> other trees lose their leaves because they slept.
> I think it's my mother's shadow that reaches him. Late
> in the day.
> *I'm so cold*, she said. *I've never been so cold.*

BROTHER

> You can't hear a photograph. That's what's holy
> about it.

SISTER

> I can hear it.
> I'm cutting the photo with my knife and fork. Yes,
> I'm eating the photograph. My father inspector and
> my mother invisible because she's the one taking the
> picture.
> She used her ironing board as a rocket.
> She sent us into space.

DEATH BED

FATHER

Do you regret being with me in the dark?

BROTHER

I have no regrets.

FATHER

Yes, you do. I hear them in your sleep.

BROTHER

How can you listen to my sleep?

FATHER

Sometimes I wake hearing ghosts of everyone who lived in the house. They leave their voices hanging on the walls.

BROTHER

Sometimes I didn't think you listened to anything.

FATHER

You get to stand by the window. Tell me what the rain looks like.

BROTHER

I told you yesterday.

FATHER

Then talk about the clouds.

TATTOO

SISTER
> Why do you have that tattoo on your arm?

BROTHER
> I got one on my back, too.

SISTER
> You can't get them off?

BROTHER
> You don't mess with tattoos.

SISTER
> Did it hurt?

BROTHER
> Yes, especially the outline—when they washed off my back with cold water, my muscles jumped.

SISTER
> My legs are tattooed with scars. I knelt down on a floor furnace at the grocer's when I was little. The grating burned through my snowsuit and skin. My bones showed.

BROTHER
> I remember your howl. OOOOUUUUUU!!

SISTER
> I was quiet with pain.
> I would like to be tattooed with the lines of one of the rocks I have. Maybe a snowflake on my breast.

BROTHER
> I don't think they tattoo there.

SISTER
> Why not?

BROTHER
> It's done with needles.

SISTER
> That gives me gooseflesh.

BROTHER
> It's what your burn marks look like.

SISTER

When have you seen them?

BROTHER

I didn't. You keep your skirt bolted down. Why did
you kneel on a fire?

SISTER

Maybe the fire called me to kneel before it.

Maybe I was trying to escape the evil queen of the
range.

Maybe I knew the road under us would always be
ice—and we'd slide over it—the walls of the house
were a fjord we were passing—one sharp call and it
would fall.

FRAGMENT

FATHER

AAOOHHH!!!

MOTHER

He should have been a vacuum-cleaner salesman. I
heard the WHOOOOOMMMMMM!!! of his motor
when he stepped into the afterlife.

PLATE VII

THE PIECE OF RED LICORICE

We'd get a treat, they told us at church. My mother sent
me to vacation Bible school. Maybe with some neighbor kids. God had a candy store where we went when
we died. We got to go there if we asked Jesus.

ROCK CONCERT

A hard mineral.

A foundation on which to stand.

Blessed be the rock.

I have a rock that looks like a fetus
all wrapped in cellophane.

I have a rock that looks like a rock.

THEIR GRAVES

They leave no bread crumbs.

The fields nearly pulled off the earth
as if Grandpa got up with a corner of the tablecloth
tucked in his pants.

I was hollowed by their spoon
a mere cantaloupe down to the green lining of the rind.
They are dead now with a gulf between us
no one can cross.

The snow there in the shadows is blue
where angels make tracks with their boots.

The whole gaudy world of the cemetery.
Trinkets of snow.
A whole night full of stars thrown out over the graves.

DANCING MAN

My sister-in-law told me my father could dance. He'd
take my mother around the floor while I was off in
another city with a husband and young children, moving on the dance floor of the bed.

How my husband danced at night, his legs jerking in
sleep as if we were on the wood floor of a dance hall,
the walls not defined but like brush beside the old
road we took back from the farm.

When I was a child, there was a Christmas party in
some dance hall. I remember the dim light, the ceiling
suspended with stars, my father's love. I remember
being small, my hands stuck in my mouth, and he
urging me out to the floor to say something to Santa
Claus, to the room full of people, to the universe itself.
To give some beautiful statement as to *why* we were all
here. And I with my shyness holding back, not going,
no, but staying by his knee.

That night was one of those times that drop you off
into the rest of life. The later realm of it anyway, iso-
lated in your own family, and you the only light it has.

Afterwards, when I was growing up, my parents never
did anything. As though my inability to speak, to carry
on the special light that was in the dance hall that
night, had darkened the room for them, too. I remember the feeling they were yoked with two children, not
especially wanting that yoke but staying with it anyway. And they were yoked with the house and the
arguments they kept behind the door of their room.
But once, when I was small, not as small as the magic
Christmas party, but a larger small, hearing my mother
cry in the bathroom, I went to see what was going on.

Where did he learn to dance? After I was gone? After my brother moved out with his wife and my mother had her days to herself and they were left alone, did they dance together again? Did the old romance come back, or was there always the feeling they faced two directions?

I remember it, too, all those years before my divorce.

The sign of deer crossing on the old highway. Yet you felt safe. You knew the deer were somewhere in the woods, but you knew you'd never see them. Yet the warnings were always there—and I did see a deer once beside the highway, maybe a buck—he stood there with my mother in the dark. She in her antlers in the bathroom, and he in the chenille bathrobe standing in the headlights.

Was there a moment my parents sighed their relief? Or did they dance all through the years and I never knew it? What does it matter? It would be too precious, too discomforting, if you could see into the hearts of parents or the man whose legs jumped beside you long after the sock hop.

I've seen the dancing—yes, that's the word. I imagine my father now in heaven with my mother and grand-parents, their wings unfolded, their haloes bobby-pinned to their heads, the great mouth of the universe smiling.

THERE HAS TO BE SOMETHING ABOUT RECONCILIATION

You know the trees lose their leaves to ease the burden of snow. But the pines hold their needles. They bear the weight of their limbs. It is a rough flight through winter. You see whole trees dropping their leaves.

The light that traveled from her hand to the sky became the moon.
On winter nights it shines through the trees that lose their leaves.

But the pines is where the moon gets lost.

FRAGMENT

There are pines in the cemetery where my parents and
grandparents are buried.
I still go there.

FRAGMENT

In this rock snow is falling.

MY EARS TUNED TO THE SPIRIT REALM

One night Grandmother Spider crept on the binding of my book, yet my hand reached instinctively and sput out the life.

The Lesser Wars

I think we have two characters here, male and female. No, I think we have one character with two parts: male and female. During the dialogue they dance the fox-trot from time to time, so the four feet of them, or the oneness of the two of them, interact.

Possibly there's no character at all, only thought.

I'm interested in the transfiguration of the word onstage. A dance of image and language. The solo of the word through a NEW DARK. And what of dramatic action? Let it go for a moment. Let it be in the twining of two bodies as though they were one.

The Lesser Wars is about a male/female relationship, as Tecoyo, the female character, says. The greater wars are what we see happening in the economy and between nations on the evening news. The male in *The Lesser Wars* has gone through a divorce and lost everything. The female has also lost in a divorce and is facing another crisis (a hysterectomy.)

They meet at the Bel-Rae Ballroom. She has just moved to Minnesota from Oklahoma. He has come to the Bel-Rae for years. She is a history teacher. It's not clear what he does. They talk, and in the act of dance, they unite. Over one summer they share their words, their mutual needs and experiences. She gives him a lesson about Columbus. He remembers his vasectomy. She tells him of her fear of surgery. He remembers his father. She remembers hers. They talk about their former spouses. They share sympathy, understanding, rage.

Their names are COYTOE and TECOYO. The Coyote tradition underpins the drama. It is a Native American myth of the Trickster, the survivor, the one who always is, the one who is always underneath what we think we are. Coytoe is a shape changer. He is the embodiment of everything (anything) (nothing), but especially of the contradictions within us.

Coytoe sticks with Tecoyo through her surgery and the loss of her idea of a child and welcomes her into her new barrenness (her discovery of the New World). He takes her to pick strawberries. He takes her to the North Shore before she teaches school again. He tells her stories, and she talks to him of what she learns as she faces the loss of the Old World. Fearing separation from Coytoe, she puts her head in a guillotine and metaphorically kills herself to become "one" with him. (It seems the woman more than the man gives up a part of herself.)

The Lesser Wars explores the risk of relationship with the *other*, the risk of knowing self, and the risk of relationship with the structure of writing.

> *The tribal trickster is a comic holotrope: the whole figuration: an unbroken interior landscape that beams various points of view in temporal reveries.*
>
> *The trickster is a comic nature in a language game, not a real person or being in the ontological sense. Tribal tricksters are embodied in imagination and liberate the mind; an androgyny, she would repudiate translations and imposed representation, as he would bare the contradiction of the striptease.*
>
> GERALD VIZENOR, *THE TRICKSTER OF LIBERTY*

YOTE CO.

Coytoe: The male of the androgynous pair.

Tecoyo: She wears a red taffeta dress, coyote ears, and sequins in her coyote fur. She carries a handfan. Dried bear ovaries and a fetus hang around her waist.

They are somewhere in their late thirties.

They sit in two chairs, the backs of which are guillotines.

A mirrored ball and red chili lights hang from the ceiling.

SORTIE I

Military music. A couple fox-trots across the floor.

TECOYO

You took me in your arms,
said,

COYTOE

Fox-trot with me, baby.
Slow. Slow. Quick-quick.

TECOYO

You counted,

COYTOE

One. Two. Three-four.

TECOYO

Our four feet moved from the burrow.

COYTOE

You were awkward at first.

TECOYO

It's just that I've had no one,
and I felt the skate blade of my chest scrape yours.
You counted,

COYTOE

One. Two. Three-four.

TECOYO

I thought you'd be like snow in Oklahoma,
gone not long after you fell.

COYTOE

But I held on.

TECOYO

You uncurled my fingers,
opened my mouth with truth.
You touched me like the jump of stones on a frozen
river
and I wondered where the anchor to your ship was.

COYTOE

I asked you to dance again and again.

TECOYO

You told me just how to follow. *(She fans coyly.)*

COYTOE

Slow. Slow. Quick-quick.

TECOYO

I held my ear next to yours,
heard the loon-call of your voice.
I looked for feathers under your arms,
moved my feet with yours.

COYTOE

Who thought the fox-trot would be our dance?

TECOYO

Who would have thought ANYTHING
would pass between the crosswalk of our hearts?

COYTOE

One. Two. Three-four.

TECOYO

But the dance floor thawed
and other continents appeared.

COYTOE

A map of Australia tattooed on your underarm.

TECOYO

I told you I was a sheep sheared in winter.

COYTOE

You're shivering. What's wrong?

TECOYO

I told you I had shearing cuts festering like strawberries.
I want to burrow—

COYTOE

I took her in my arms.
Licked her wounds.
What else could I do with a part of myself?
And a piece of land white as the frozen ground at my
window.

TECOYO

(Eyes closed. Dreamily.)

Right. Two-three.
Left. Two-three.
COYTOE
  Why were you alone?
  A prEEty thing like you?
TECOYO
  I moved here by myself.
  For a long time, I sat alone in the evenings
  drinking my cup of black tea
  and shriveling to a walnut.
  Then I came to the Bel-Rae Ballroom.
COYTOE
  What do you do?
TECOYO
  Teach.
COYTOE
  What do you teach?
TECOYO
  History.
COYTOE
  Yipe-os.
  I don't know anything about the past.
  Did you leave a lover behind when you moved?
TECOYO
  No.
  What don't you know about the past?
COYTOE
  The first moment you pushed nose against mine.
TECOYO
  I don't know what happened then either, Coytoe.
  I forgot the sheep shivering in Australia, I guess.
COYTOE
  I like your fan.
TECOYO
  See the azaleas on it?
  I've always wanted a garden with geraniums and
  petunias.

Trillium.
Blue phlox.
Zinnias.

COYTOE

Chee-O!
You really do like flowers.
Come with me to the North Shore.
There are wildflowers—

TECOYO

(She interrupts.) I've always had this cabin in my mind.
This place—
But I don't know where it is.

COYTOE

We'll go over July 4th.

TECOYO

I can't.

COYTOE

We get along so well.
It's like we're both a part of one.

TECOYO

I have that feeling, too.
But I can't.

COYTOE

(Fingering her fan.) Why not?
I'd show you the wildflowers.

TECOYO

I'll tell you when I know for sure.

COYTOE

(Exploring further.) What are these at your waist?

TECOYO

Dried bear ovaries and a fetus. Just the idea of a child,
really. I couldn't decide whether to have one or not.

COYTOE

You're about to run out of time, Tecoyo.

TECOYO

You're speaking more truth than you know. I want

a child. I've always wanted one. I've written a
composition called, "My Child": He runs through the
field. He catches butterflies. He makes a chain of summer flowers.

COYTOE

And the berries? *(He looks at them.)*

TECOYO

Dried bear ovaries. The part of me that wants to
remain barren. The part of me that's the "Warrhameh"
—the war woman who wears the ovaries against conception. I don't really want to be pregnant. The terrible
responsibility, you know. It's the male in me, I guess.

COYTOE

Now, wait—

TECOYO

Oh, I've had so many friends who don't receive child
support. The poor women hold it all together.

COYTOE

I always pay what I owe. Most of it, anyway.

TECOYO

Now my choice is being made for me. I think I'm
going to have to have surgery.

COYTOE

What kind?

TECOYO

A hysterectomy.

COYTOE

That's the reason you can't go to the North Shore?

TECOYO

Yes.

COYTOE

Are you sure? The lake is like a dance floor—

TECOYO

I've got two opinions and they both say the same.

COYTOE

We can go later in the summer, then. What's wrong?

TECOYO

> It's my old hurts festering like strawberries. The fallopian tubes and ovaries are just like ripe strawberries before they're picked. I saw pictures of them in a pamphlet the doctor gave me and I said, "strawberries."

COYTOE

> I like to pick strawberries. I go to J & L Farms. You want to come with me sometime?

TECOYO

> Sure.

SORTIE II

TECOYO

> I open the shoe box of myself.
> Not just cardboard marked with size and brand
> but filled with tongue and sole.
> I paint my face.
> The egg of my lovesick heart in the wicker basket of
> my ribs.
> I sigh like an army bugle.
> There are times I want some coyote to hold me.
> I want to feel his chest against mine.
> Then he'll go off to someone else.
> They're all such tricksters.
> Even me.
> Wasn't I married once?
> Wasn't I as far away as Australia?
> Didn't I hurt like a flock of sheep?
> How long did I want out?
> There's more than my body when I move.
> A rich field of wildflowers and a MIND.
> If only they knew.
> But I'm headless to them.
> Only the part between my hind legs counts.
> I always get caught in a snowstorm,
> the claws of mascara down my face.

COYTOE

> *(He combs his chest hair.)*
> A man needs a woman.
> It's how I prefer to take care of my hard-on.
> Sex. That's the first thing.
> Then I need a woman to need me.
> I like for her to like me.
> I know sex means more to a woman.
> She gets emotionally involved.

I understand that.
So I'm careful with her.
I would sleep around but she'd find out.
So I curb my appetite for others
for now anyway.
She's not bad.
The colors in her eyes are lovely—
the way gasoline floats on a puddle.
I could do worse.
So it's back to the Bel-Rae Ballroom.

SORTIE III

COYTOE

Fox-trot with me, baby.

TECOYO

(Fanning) I'm going to have a hysterectomy.

COYTOE

Will it interfere with this dance?

TECOYO

No, it's not for another month. I have to teach summer
school.

They dance.

COYTOE

You're missing the steps again.

TECOYO

Then count for me.

COYTOE

One. Two. Three-four.

Slow. Slow. Quick-quick.

TECOYO

I'm always awkward at first.

COYTOE

You've got other things on your mind.

TECOYO

Summer school for one.

COYTOE

A hysterectomy for another.

TECOYO

The world to Columbus was Europe, Asia, Africa.
North. South. East. The West was closed until three
ships sailed toward it. Three directions in search of the
fourth.

COYTOE

There's always four directions.

Up. Down. Back. Forth.

TECOYO

> Then Columbus went forth.

COYTOE

> Like I'm going after you? *(His hand creeps across her breast.)*

TECOYO

> *(She moves his hand.)* You get me lost now where I'm at.
> Let me tell my story.
> I teach history, remember?
>
> Columbus thought it was smaller than it was:
> the earth.

COYTOE

> Is this your "Composition on Columbus"?

Tecoyo ignores his question.

> One. Two. Three-four.

TECOYO

> He thought it was smaller than it was: the earth.
> And Asia larger.
> Only a handspan across the water.
> West. By God, he'd sail it.

Coytoe's hand tries to move across her breast again, but she pushes it away.

> It was his vision-quest
> in the wilderness of the waves.
> A roller-coaster ride.
> Up. Down.

Tecoyo makes exaggerated movements with her arms as they dance.

COYTOE

> The *Pinta, Niña, Santa María*
> fox-troting on the waves.

TECOYO

> This's MY story.

COYTOE

> Three fleas on the sea.
> One. Two-three.
> You're missing steps again.

TECOYO

How could three ships cross a rocky sea five hundred
years ago?

COYTOE

How could covered wagons cross America?
How can ANYTHING happen, given the odds?
But—"Ah!" Columbus said, "Land ho!"

TECOYO

Not yet!
I teach this, remember?
The Atlantic is hardly under them and the little arsenal
of boats tossed—

COYTOE

Slow. Slow. Quick-quick.

TECOYO

Oh, I don't want to dance.
I want to talk about boats on an open sea.

She continues her story while he dances on.

How else could the continents come together?

*(She works an imaginary crank and does other corny gestures as
she speaks.)*

I teach pictorial history.
In other words, I ACT OUT history.
I make it travel—

COYTOE

All this and she can almost dance, too.

TECOYO

*(Overly dramatic. She speaks as a teacher sold on her own ability
to present her information.)*

1492:
Aug 3 eighty-eight men weighed anchor in the little
fleet
Aug 6 the *Pinta* lost her rudder and they turned back
for repair
Sept 6 they tried again
Sept 13 variations of the magnetic needle were observed

Sept 15 a meteor fell into the sea about five leagues
away
Sept 17 the men began to murmur, frightened because
they couldn't always find west

COYTOE

No more chance than three fleas on the face of the
moon.

TECOYO

Sept 18 they saw birds and a ridge of low clouds
Sept 20 they still expected land, and Columbus had
difficulty keeping his men encouraged
Sept 25 the cry of land! (but it proved false)
Oct 7 more disappointment
Oct 11 the *Pinta* fished up a pole which looked man
made
Oct 12 appearance of the New World!

COYTOE

Ah! Land.

TECOYO

That same day Columbus and his crew kneeled on the
shore. They all gave thanks to God, kissing the ground
with tears for the great mercy they had received.
Columbus had found the New World.

COYTOE

It was all theirs for the taking.

SORTIE IV

TECOYO

We're picking strawberries at the J & L Farms *(Pause)*—
before the surgery, after we were getting along.

COYTOE

I'll be with you. Do you think I'd let you go through
that alone?

TECOYO

We just met. How can I expect you to do that for me?

COYTOE

It didn't take long to know you were a part of me. You
don't have anyone else.

TECOYO

The rows of strawberries are telling their tales.
The red testicles of them in the green frames of leaves.
As I pick the strawberries
their red portraits bleed.
I'm ready to go to the sky, and you said,

COYTOE

Fox-trot with me, baby.

TECOYO

I want to be with my family again. And they're all
dead. I want to see my father. I've thought about him
lately. See, out across the field, the people with their
buckets. All of us are only here momentarily. For a
morning. Standing in our summer dresses and trousers
in the middle of the field. We're all migrant workers.
Filling our boxes with red fruit. Luscious strawberries.
The little ovaries of them, red and diseased.

COYTOE

One. Two. Three-four.

TECOYO

I want to go. I remember my father in the basement.
Back in the early days when I was small and hunker-
ing beside him on the basement floor as he skinned

pheasant & quail. Rabbit & deer. I was a part of him
then. I waited for him to get back from his hunting
trips. He named the animals for me. We thanked them
for their lives. I was part of the universe when I was
with him. He was Adam with the old Indian language
wedged in his teeth.

COYTOE

My father was a wedge in my teeth.

TECOYO

My mother's dead too. Most of the family—except
my brother. I don't want to stay here without them—I
could be myself when I was with them—with my husband, I felt I had to be what he wanted.
I think it's easier there—

COYTOE

You can't go like that.

TECOYO

Yes I can.

COYTOE

I told you I'd be with you.

TECOYO

I'm going over the edge of the earth.
Who will go with me?

COYTOE

Not I, said the coyote.
I'm staying here long as I can.

TECOYO

Then I'll go myself.

COYTOE

You're making too much of this.

TECOYO

I belong to the Flat Earth Society.
It's a group for women.
It's what men have always done to us.
Saying we'll fall off if we go too far.
Maybe that's where my cabin is—
the place I've always dreamed of.

COYTOE

It'll be a piece of cake.

Don't worry, Tecoyo.

I mean—Sweetie—

I had a vasectomy.

TECOYO

You can't compare that to a hysterectomy.

You wear your genitals on your elbow.

Mine are INSIDE!

COYTOE

A piece of cake.

I was on the table watching—

TECOYO

You watched the doctor cut into your testicles!

COYTOE

I asked if I could—

TECOYO

EOOOOOWW!

COYTOE

He gave me a local anesthetic.

He made two incisions in my balls with a little knife.

He fished around for the two cords

and pulled them out.

Tecoyo is going through contortions.

They looked like spaghetti.

Homemade spaghetti.

TECOYO

AAAAHHHHHHHHH!

COYTOE

He tied the cords with surgical thread and cut them

with scissors.

Then he tucked them neatly back

and sewed up the incisions.

I went home holding an ice pack to my crotch.

Boy did I have balls for awhile—

Bright Christmas-tree ornaments.

Giant blue strawberries for your box.
Some men get impotent afterwards—
Psychological.
But I could fuck anything.

TECOYO

I'm sure your wife appreciated that.

COYTOE

I was faithful to her for awhile—
Until I couldn't cut the crap.
She wouldn't talk.
I didn't want to be with her anymore.
She kept the house.
The kids. The car.
The bank account.
The egg timer.

TECOYO

You still didn't get your balls and penis cut off.
That's what a hysterectomy is.

COYTOE

Not exactly, Sweet Pea.
You can still get fucked.

SORTIE V

COYTOE

If I could've been out of there, I would have.
But I'm a Trickster, doing what no one expects.
Even myself—

I need this? I kept asking.
My X took me for what I had.
I didn't have anything left
but oatmeal to eat for supper.

Women were going to be for pleasure from now on.
Nothing else.
But I saw the July 4th fireworks in Tecoyo's eyes.
I licked her wounds.
I held her hand and thought:
all of us are in this life,
this parade
we don't know how we got in.

The spirit of Christopher Columbus himself
took hold of me
and I sailed for the New World.

Ah! LOVE.
Like a Riceroni boxtop.
The beep of a cable car—
or a storm warning across the bottom of the TV screen.
But I'm a coyote.
A Trickster tricked as often as I trick.
How long can I be expected to stay in one place?

But I look at that school-teacher and think,
I'm the margin on your papers, baby.
The space between the lines.

You want to be me, baby?—
Ms. Warrhameh?—Warrior Woman.

Just listen and you'll be glad
you're what you are:

The Trickster is always fighting himself.
When he goes hunting
his right arm struggles with his left
and he maims himself.

And you say you stay by yourself
drinking your black walnut tea?
Doesn't it bother you?

TECOYO
I didn't really have a choice.

COYTOE
You do now, baby.
If you can cut the rug.
If you can live like this.
Then you're in Coyote-land.

TECOYO
Eternal Trickster.
Earlier stage of consciousness.

What we are out on the ocean in a tiny ship?
What we are when no one sees?

COYTOE
How we are intertwined in sameness.

TECOYO
We put on the Trickster
what we need to shuck in order
to move on to a higher civilization.

COYTOE
Yet we can't forget who we were.
We're still fascinated by that part of ourselves.

TECOYO
Fox-trot with me, baby.

COYTOE
I'm impossible to hold.
Yet I'm always here.

SORTIE VI

TECOYO

Whenever I take off down the runway in a plane, I'll
think of the morning I was wheeled into surgery. The
day after summer school, Coytoe took me to the hospital at 5:30 in the last of the dark before dawn. It's
always when I *know* the earth is flat. We parked the car
and walked through the doors that opened toward us.
I went to a desk down the hall and filled out papers.
They took me into a room where I took off my clothes
and put on a hospital gown that opened down the
back. They took my temp & blood. I answered their
questions and went to the bathroom and waited. They
lead me to a row of gurneys, and I got up on one of
them. I shivered, and they put socks on my feet and
covered me. A nurse came and put an IV in my wrist.
She said the needle had Novocain in it and it wouldn't
hurt. The hospital minister came and talked to me—
Death where is your sting? I waited. The anesthesiologist
came and told me he'd administer the anesthesia
through my IV. I was wheeled down a long runway
into the surgery room.

COYTOE

A piece of cake.

TECOYO

Everyone was getting ready for what they would do.
No one seemed to notice I was there idling beside
them. Soon they transferred me from the gurney to
the operating table. Then everything was gone and
I soloed in the dark for awhile.

Maybe it was more like an old instrument flight.

Aug 6 The *Pinta* lost her rudder—

COYTOE

A piece of cake.

TECOYO

In recovery, when I landed, there was an oxygen mask
on my face. It was steamy and I was cold. A nurse said
they'd take me to my room. Out in the hall, Coytoe
leaned over me. *(She looks at him.)* "I'd been wondering
where you were," I said.

COYTOE

My one foot wanted to leave.

But my other foot stayed.

TECOYO

We went up an elevator, and I must have slept again. I
heard someone say they were going to transfer me to
my bed. They slid a board under me, and I was in bed
in my hospital room.

COYTOE

A piece of jelly roll.

TECOYO

It was quiet again. I slept on & off. I felt pain. The
nurses came in for blood pressure & temp. In the afternoon they tried to get me up. I felt sick to my stomach,
but I had nothing to throw up. The nurse gave me a
shot for nausea and another one for pain. My brother
called from Oklahoma, but my voice was hoarse and I
couldn't say much. It was because of the tube that had
been in my throat during surgery. The nurses came to
change my IV and empty the urine bag. My temp went
up to 101 the first night. The doctor said my lungs were
congested. I tried to cough for them, but it hurt too
much. They pushed a pillow against my stomach and
said it would be easier to cough, but it wasn't. I felt a
burst of fireworks on July 4th in my stomach. I got more
shots for the pain and felt my body fall back into sleep.
Then they took the catheter out and I struggled to uri-
nate, but couldn't. My hand swelled from the IV and I
begged them to take it out. Finally, they did.

COYTOE

Definitely a piece of crumb cake.

TECOYO

For two days they brought jello squares, shiny as
polyurethane, and yellowed chicken broth, and I said
even if I felt good it would make me sick. I wanted
something to eat. I started passing gas. That's all they
asked me for two days. Had I passed gas? I couldn't
eat until things were going through. If I got plugged up,
I'd know what discomfort was. Was I coughing every
opportunity I could? Was I breathing into the little
machine they brought? Did I want pneumonia? My
temp was high, and I shivered. I felt sick and wondered
if I would live. My father hadn't survived surgery. I
could let this sickness take me in its mouth and drag
me to its cave. I could die after all. I had it in my power.
What if my bladder never worked again? *(Tecoyo puts
her hand to her face.)* I felt my fingers wiggle and strange
shadows passed in my head. I felt at times I was leaving. *(Coytoe puts his arm around her.)* Coytoe pulled me
out of bed and walked me to the door of the room.

The next day, I walked down the hall hanging onto
him. I couldn't even stand up straight. I thought he
would talk about cake. I thought he would say,
"Fox-trot with me, baby."

But he just walked beside me—

Later in the night, I thought "Welcome to the New
World."

(Pause.)

I was catheterized four times.

COYTOE

If I could've been out of there—

TECOYO

That really means eight:
in out
in out
in out
in out

(She juts her hand back and forth.)

> The stiff little tube
> up the urethra into the bladder.
> The little balloon holding it in.
> The hook to the bag of urine in my hand
> as I walked.
>
> The last time I was catheterized,
> I couldn't sleep.
> That night in the hospital, I saw a cross on the ceiling.
> There was a car in the drive before dawn.
> Its lights through the window made a cross.
> I watched it for awhile.
> Then the car moved from the driveway
> and the cross was gone.

COYTOE

> My favorite part was the staples on her stomach
> like a jagged, silver zipper.

TECOYO

> Do they hurt when they come out?

COYTOE

> Oh, no.
> Nothing hurts here.
> The ends are not bent like regular staples.
> They'll come right out.

TECOYO

> They pulled the catheter right out.
> "Take a deep breath," they'd say.
>
> Then I struggled to urinate and couldn't.
>
> When my abdomen grew hard with urine
> they'd come back with another package.
> I watched them unwrap the bag and the long tube.
> I watched them insert the stick into the tube.
>
> They put a plastic sheet under me
> and spread my legs.

I held the bed rails with my hands
and thought of escape.

They separated my lips
and cleaned with a wipe.

They stuck the tube in SLOWLY
all the way UP the steps to the sky.

"Here comes the urine," they said.
They pulled the sheet out from under me
with some red antiseptic smeared on it.
They wadded up the cellophane wrapping
and threw it all away.

I stayed in bed
with the tube poked against my spine,
the urethra stinging like a wasp caught in it.

"Visualize," the nurse said.
And I did.
There was a time of drought in Israel, and Elijah saw a
small cloud on the horizon, and he said, "Rain." Every
time a little splat hit, I said, "rain," and finally one
morning there was rain.
A little at a time.
But I got to go home.

It was an empty cross I saw on the ceiling that night.
He had risen for me.

But I had the feeling someone still had to die.
COYTOE
    Not me, said the coyote.
TECOYO
    Drive slow, Coytoe.
    But keep heading away from here.

When I sleep I dream I'm being held down.
I am the one who will be the sacrifice.
Jesus, where are you?
Who are these thieves standing over me?

She thrashes with her arms. Coytoe tries to hold her.

COYTOE

> Now don't get hysterical.
> Isn't that why women have hysterectomies?

> Count backwards.
> Four-three. Two. One.
> Quick-quick. Slow. Slow.

TECOYO

> Four-three. Two. One.

> Look, how lovely—the uterus and fallopian tubes are
> something like a small, winged bird. Or a marsh fern
> with graceful, spiky stalks. The ovaries dance like
> grateful strawberries. But NOW my Indian name is
> Warrhameh.

COYTOE

(Coytoe unties the fetus.)

> Now the fetus.

TECOYO

> No.

COYTOE

> Yes. It's dead.

*Tecoyo tries to hold on to it while Coytoe tries to get it away
from her.*

TECOYO

> NO!!

*Coytoe pulls the fetus away from her and beheads it on the guillo-
tine of his chair.*

> We could have picked wildflowers in a field.
> I could have shown you how the ants march in a row.
> You could have shown me life.

SORTIE VII

COYTOE
I remember pheasant hunting with my father.
Walking through the cornfield in autumn.
We didn't have dogs
and the birds would stay in the rows
between the corn as long as they had cover.
We'd walk back and forth across the field,
moving toward one end to flush them out.
They'd fly when they got to the clearing
at the end of the field
and we'd shoot,
always leading them with the shotgun.

When I saw the bird I shot—
How beautiful he was—his amber feathers
speckled with brown and white and yellow—
his long tail feathers and red warrior face—
the white ring around his neck—
I thought someone far away had dressed him
and sent him here.
Why had I shot him?

I felt—
the first time—
You know when else I felt like that?
When the girl down the road—
wearing a necklace and overalls—
When I asked her to unbuckle her overalls—
and I saw the moon-print of her navel—
and the private seam—
like a hard peach before it's ripe—

I couldn't shoot pheasant anymore.
My father called me, "Berdache—"

TECOYO

A man who's become a woman.

But that's not true, Coytoe.

COYTOE

Good old father. If he could hold us in his hand, he could make us smaller. He wrapped us in the chicken wire of his cruelty. He bound our heads so our thoughts wouldn't grow. He had us, yes. He lead us with the shotgun of his ridicule.

SORTIE VIII

TECOYO
> My former husband and I went to a cabin in
> Oklahoma once.
> Waves lapped on the shore.
> Back. Forth. Back. Forth.
> I wanted to go to the bedroom first off.
> But HE brought in the groceries, the suitcases.
>
> In the kitchen
> there was a small table with the paint cracked
> like spirit-signs on an Indian vase.
> All along the crack marks,
> the spirits were trying to get out.
>
> The whole cabin leaned toward the back,
> where the bedroom was.
> But he sat on the porch with his feet on the rail.
>
> The warped cabin
> with its little print curtains,
> the walls and floor following the curvature of the earth.
>
> The little waves spilling
> into the shore like a climax.

COYTOE
> What did your husband do for work?

TECOYO
> He was a flooring man.
> Carpets and linoleum.
> Hardwood when he could sell it.
>
> I felt I lost a part of my life when I was with him.
> Will I lose my life to be with you?

COYTOE
> Of course not, Tecoyo. No one loses their life here.

TECOYO
> Well, I thumbed through the bird book he brought.

The first page I turned to
was the yellow-rumped warbler.
COYTOE
My X's mother braided rugs.
She was always looking for scraps of cloth.
TECOYO
That afternoon
the trees were full of warblers & waxwings & grosbeaks.
Twee-twee-twee.
To-whee.
Cleep-cleep.
Thieef-thieef.

This is my composition called, "The Birds."
COYTOE
I was afraid to leave my shirt on the back of a chair.
TECOYO
Whether you are in the city
or on the north lake shore
of SUPERIOR
you will derive HOURS + HOURS of pleasure
from birds.
COYTOE
My X hasn't kept the house up like she should.
I even made a barbecue pit in the backyard
which she let go to hell.
Coyote in a chef's apron!
What a suburban fuck!
TECOYO
When you see a new and unfamiliar bird,
what points should you notice in naming him?
Overall, is the bird slim or chunky?
Is his neck long or short?
Is his tail forked at the tip?
Or is it round? Or pointed?
Is his beak straight or curved?
When the bird flies,

does he leave you with a hollowness as big as the sky
squatting down to touch the lake?

COYTOE

I even made a patio.

I think she rented a jackhammer—

TECOYO

Birds make two kinds of noises.

Songs and calls.

The songs are for a mate in breeding season.

The calls express alarm or maintain contact

so the bird won't be alone.

(She makes a bird noise.)

COYTOE

I think you're in the breeding season. *(He is trying to
skip stones across the water.)*

TECOYO

No. I just don't want to feel alone—

COYTOE

What do you think we have together?

TECOYO

A relationship—

COYTOE

—between a man and woman—

TECOYO

The lesser wars.

Until we get tired of one another

and you find someone else. *(She fans herself.)*

The greater wars, I suppose, are among nations.

COYTOE

What if you find someone else?

TECOYO

It's usually the male that leaves.

That's part of my "Bird" composition also.

But there's something more.

I'm not sure yet—I found that as we grew together,

I was more like him.

We could change places—
Not that he was a she.
But he became dependent on me in a way.
I was part-him after all and he was part-she.
We were one coyote looking at another.

I want my spirit to get out from beneath the cracked
paint of my face.
I want to FLY over the edge of the earth to the sun.
What if we could reach the sun like Icarus?

COYTOE

You'd be a well-done coyote.
Fried rice, baby.
Charred charisma.

TECOYO

I'd be FREED rice.
I'd know the fullness of the light.

COYTOE

You'd be white lightness itself.

TECOYO

That's what I'd be.

COYTOE

That's why we have wax wings on our heels, baby.
The doors to paradise are closed.
We can't get there from here.
Not in ourselves as we are.
We'd pollute it anyway,
just like we have the land we discovered
and ourselves.

TECOYO

We'd be pure and serene.

COYTOE

We'd be dead—

TECOYO

—to ourselves and others.

COYTOE

Why didn't you and your husband have children?

TECOYO

I guess I didn't think the marriage would hold water,
much less children. Conception didn't happen. Maybe
I always felt kinked. *(Tecoyo holds her stomach.)*

COYTOE

How long were you married?

TECOYO

Nine years.

COYTOE

Fox-trot with me, baby.
One. Two. Three-four.
Slow. Slow. Quick-quick.

TECOYO

I thought you'd be like snow in Oklahoma.

COYTOE

But I held on.

TECOYO

Why am I so happy right now?
What's wrong?
Isn't life for suffering?

They fox-trot again to the military music.

SORTIE IX

TECOYO

(She fans herself.)

> In the night, your watch looked like an open mouth
> with little, sharp teeth.

COYTOE

> The illuminated markers around the dial—

TECOYO

> I thought I was being devoured by a rodent.
> If you hurt me, you hurt yourself, you know.

COYTOE

> I'll take my watch off at night.

TECOYO

> You opened my mouth with truth.

COYTOE

> You want truth?
> Let me be first, then.
> I have a friend who asked me to go to the Bel-Rae
> Ballroom with her this week.
> I told her I couldn't, but she insisted.
> You're not really feeling well yet.
> You're up and down all night like the flag on a ship.

TECOYO

> I still have trouble urinating.

COYTOE

> I didn't think you'd mind—

TECOYO

> I do.
> But it has to be that way.
> We should be able to pick strawberries where we want.
> I might have a friend I want to go out with now &
> then. But for now
> you just want to dance with another woman.

COYTOE

> Remember the relationship we agreed on?

TECOYO
> Yes, I've known it all my life.
> I'm supposed to be faithful
> and you can do what you like.
> I was married too many years.
> I know exactly how that works.

COYTOE
> You can't expect to smother me.

TECOYO
> I would like to do more than that.

COYTOE
> I thought you could handle this.

TECOYO
> Handle what? Getting left behind?
> I don't like this new shore.
> You're tired of me.

COYTOE
> Not yet, Tecoyo.
> But keep pushing—
> A coyote doesn't wear a leash.

TECOYO
> Whatever you say, dear.

COYTOE
> You're afraid you're not attractive to me—
> Because you've got a scar like a man's fly on your
> stomach.

TECOYO
> How do I live with my new self?
> The old one left so quickly.
> What did they do to me?
> What if I can't love again?
> It's the last thing I feel like now.

COYTOE
> You'll be able to love.

TECOYO
> But in the meantime, partner,
> you go to the Bel-Rae Ballroom—

Have a good time, dear.
Don't worry about me.
It's all right if I'm sick.

COYTOE

I had a gal get sick in my car once.
My red Ford Torino.
I called it "The Red Raper."
It was all I had after the divorce.
She'd invited me to a Christmas party.
She ate too many hors d'oeuvres
and drank too much wine.
On the way home she said she felt sick.
She didn't even roll down the window.

TECOYO

Yeeks.
What did you do?

COYTOE

I just kept driving—
It was everywhere so quick.
I cleaned it up the next day.
It was in between the cracks in the seat.
It was on the floor—
the dash—
the window and door.
I mean, she just went—

TECOYO

AARRGH!

COYTOE

I tried to air the Torino out.
It must have been 30 below.

SORTIE X

TECOYO
> I keep having dreams.
> I start school again soon—

COYTOE
> Back to three boats sailing the Atlantic.

TECOYO
> I don't feel good. Maybe that's it.

COYTOE
> Go to the doctor.

TECOYO
> I am.
> I keep remembering the hospital minister saying,
> we die—or what if we die?
> I don't remember exactly what he said
> when he visited me the morning of surgery.
> But he sure talks now in my dreams.
> I saw a cross on the ceiling of the hospital room.
> I see it again when I dream.
> It isn't just from car headlights in the drive,
> but it's the shadow of a larger cross—
> A ladder to heaven.
> There are birds flying toward it
> with wings like fallopian tubes
> and eyes like strawberries.
> The whole world is a bloody hysterectomy
> with jellied organs on the table,
> slippery as icy roads in Minnesota.
>
> You stood with me when the nurse picked out
> my staples, Coytoe.
> You've seen my scar.
> You've seen my shaved part.
> I'm so close to you sometimes I feel I am you.
> Yet there's a gulf between us.

COYTOE

> We can't own one another.
>
> Though sometimes I think we can *be* one another.

TECOYO

> This is my syllogism:
>
> It is cold in Minnesota.
>
> We are in Minnesota.
>
> Therefore we are frigid.

COYTOE

> No—You've helped me forget some of my bitterness.
>
> Maybe I'm becoming human.
>
> Is that the final trick I play on myself?
>
> I keep having dreams, too. Sometimes I wake at night
> with the biggest hard-on I've ever had. I see you lying
> flat on the bed with your legs spread like the wings of
> some angelic bird that will take me to heaven.

TECOYO

> You want wings?
>
> You want to fly?

COYTOE

> I mount you and part the curtain to the high country
> where it's hard to catch our breath. I'm riding the
> waves, all right—riding and riding until the waves
> wash up on land.

TECOYO

> I dream of that gulf between us.
>
> I enter it alone.
>
> I become something else also.
>
> The minister says, we are killed all the day long,
> we are counted as sheep for the slaughter.
>
> I die daily—I can't be me anymore.
>
> I lost the child I wanted to have.

COYTOE

> He was just an idea.

TECOYO

> I lost the part of me with wings.

Tecoyo opens a pill bottle. Coytoe reads the label.

COYTOE
> Sulfamethox.

TECOYO
> It's the sulfur I take for a bladder infection, and I had
> an allergic reaction. I started to itch. I couldn't scratch
> myself enough.
> A rash crawled up my bright red scar. It went in my
> ears, the back of my throat. It raged over my body in
> skirmishes.

COYTOE
> Let me take you to the hospital, my speckled friend.

TECOYO
> No. They'd put an IV in my arm.
> It would flood my body.
> Then they'd catheterize me—
> A battalion of them are waiting at the door with their
> tubes—

COYTOE
> Your skin is like fry bread just out of the skillet—

TECOYO
> My tongue feels like it has a bone in it.

COYTOE
> I want to take you to the hospital.

TECOYO
> *(She talks with a raspy voice.)* NO!
> Go back to sleep.
> I'll be brave and put my head on the line.

(Tecoyo lays her head on the chair under the guillotine.)

> I felt the shearing cuts when my husband took off for
> Australia.
> I feel the death-dance of the histamines sucking my
> body.

COYTOE
> Slurp.

TECOYO
> All night in a rain-soaked tent
> the motorcade of tank and jeep hiss by.

Tell me, general, how long do we have in the
trenches—

COYTOE

Slurp.

TECOYO

I'll tell you something, Coytoe—

I think it was over the moment Columbus landed.

COYTOE

Slurp.

SORTIE XI

TECOYO
> You know how you'll be going somewhere
> and someplace far away comes to mind?—
> A back-road curve in Osage County,
> or the flat highway to Seiling, Oklahoma.
> I see those places when we dance
> at the Bel-Rae Ballroom.

COYTOE
> One. Two. Three-four.
> Slow. Slow. Quick-quick.

TECOYO
> I see the short-grass prairie when I drive—
> But I don't want to be there.
> I want to be here dancing with you—
> My spirit flying from the cracked paint on my face.

COYTOE
> I think you should rest awhile.

TECOYO
> Who do you want to dance with?

COYTOE
> That's not it. You've been sick.
> I think you should rest.

TECOYO
> Whatever you say, dear—
> All right. I'll rest.
> I feel light-headed anyway.
> But you dance—

Coytoe circles the dance floor.

> Don't worry about me.
> You just do what you want.
> You back out of the drive in your big red Torino,
> leave me with a bladder infection.
> Don't bother about me.

Look how much bigger your hand is than mine.
Your brain must be the size of your carburetor.
I'll watch you dance.
I'll clean the carp you catch.
I'll chop wood for your trip to the North Shore.
I'll just wait in a snowstorm, dear.

SORTIE XII

COYTOE
> This is my composition called, "The Loon."

(He puts his finger in her ear.)

TECOYO

(Hits his hand away.)

> You can't write a composition.
> I'm the teacher, remember?
> And I start school next week.

COYTOE
> The loons are left over from a primitive water bird.

TECOYO
> The lake is like a dance floor for angels under the sky.
> I'm glad we came to the North Shore, Coytoe.

COYTOE
> I've wanted to come all summer.

TECOYO
> The fog has finally cleared. The waves stick up like
> little razors. Anyone else would gash their feet.

COYTOE
> The present-day loon has no close relatives among
> modern birds.

TECOYO
> *(She puts her fingers in her ears.)* This is my composition
> called, "The Cold."

COYTOE
> The loon's heavy solid bones help him dive underwater.
> On still nights, the lake shores ring with the loon's
> hair-raising call. *(He mimics a loon call.)*

TECOYO
> *(Ignoring him)* My composition is written on the North
> Shore on Labor Day.
> It says that Minnesota is cold. Not user-friendly.

COYTOE

The loon has a black-and-white checkerboard pattern on its upperparts. *(He pats his chest.)* The loon has a velvety black head. *(He smooths his head with his hand.)* The loon has a white necklace. (He looks at Tecoyo.) White underparts. Wow!

TECOYO

I could write a composition called, "When 12 degrees Is a Warm Spell." It would not be about the weather. *(She looks at him.)*

COYTOE

The loon has a straight, black daggerlike bill and RED COYOTE EYES!

TECOYO

I don't like your composition.

COYTOE

He makes loud yodeling calls in the breeding grounds. *(He makes another loon call.)*

TECOYO

There are questions you could ask yourself:
Why am I irritating her?

COYTOE

There are questions you could ask yourself.
Why is he still here?

TECOYO

Your name is Coytoe. Mine, Tecoyo. We're both forms of Coyote—a play of the imagination.

COYTOE

A trip to what we have here—is a risk. I want to arrive at someplace I've never been. I want new land—If you see it as a dance—a voyage to a new world. Maybe not THE New World—but another continent.

TECOYO

Yes, you would like it that way.

COYTOE

You are a new world for me, Tecoyo. You aren't the *only* world, but the one I've found.

I let my anchor down over the edge of my ship—
I felt it touch bottom—
I feel it belong—

TECOYO

You're no more than the fits and starts of a small fleet
on an ocean that could swallow it.

COYTOE

What if I'm here longer than you think?

TECOYO

What if it comes to its usual end?

COYTOE

A mother-in-law cutting up my clothes
to make braided rugs.
But I'm a Trickster with many tales.

TECOYO

Spare me at least half of them.

COYTOE

Trickster went hunting. He tricked a buffalo into a
muddy trough. Immediately the Trickster was on him
with his knife and killed him.

*Coytoe pokes at Tecoyo as he talks, taunting her. She tries to stop
him. His right arm holds off her left arm.*

The Trickster dragged the buffalo to the woods and
skinned him. All the while using his right arm, when
suddenly his left arm grabbed the buffalo. *(In a high
voice)* "It's mine," said the left arm. "Stop that or I'll
use my knife on you," the right arm answered. The left
arm released its hold. But soon it grabbed the buffalo
again. The right arm repeated the same threat. Again
and again both of Trickster's arms argued. The quarrel
soon turned into a vicious fight, and the left arm was
badly cut. "Why do I do this?" Trickster asked himself.
"I have made myself suffer."

TECOYO

Put it in a zip-lock bag and move on.

COYTOE
> How about the one where Trickster took an elk liver
> and made a vulva from it. Then he put on a dress—

TECOYO
> I don't want to hear your Trickster stories.

COYTOE
> I haven't told you what he did with the fox—
>
> I haven't read you Coyote's composition on flowers:
> Azaleas.
> Blue phlox.
> Hollyhocks.

TECOYO
> You want a composition?
> How about another one on truth?
>
> Well—
> This is my composition on truth.
> You opened my mouth with it.
>
> I'm evolving, too
> into whatever comes next.
> I'm sailing west.
> There's a place I've always wanted—
> a cabin somewhere over the edge of the earth.
>
> We're whole
> when we're the trinity and us—
> It's the 4-cornered pledge
> we take at the Flat Earth Society.
>
> But I lost my rudder on the way.
> Meteors fall like snow.

COYTOE
> You think you lost your way?
>
> I lost more than mine.
> The X gets half my salary.
> She claims the kids.
> I have to live in a one-bedroom apartment

on the poverty level.
She has the power because of the courts.
I have no options.
No power.
Could I get married on half of what I make?
That's what I had to live on for years.
TECOYO
The ocean's shiny as formica.
Little waves HISS.
A new land waits somewhere.
Who will help me navigate?
COYTOE
Not I, said the coyote. I'm staying here.
TECOYO
Then I'll go myself.
COYTOE
One Christmas she was supposed to bring the kids
over at noon.
We agreed.
I made dinner for them.
At one it was ready.
At three it was dried out.
At five I threw it away.
At eight she called and asked if she could bring them.
I said, "NO!"
I had waited the whole day.
The frustration erupted—
I yelled at her on the phone.
(Coytoe shouts in a rage.) "You father fucker."
I kicked the Christmas presents.
I hit the walls.
God damn the injustice of it!
TECOYO
Four-three. Two. One.
Glide-glide. Two. One.
(Tecoyo comforts him.) Count backwards—it's all right.

COYTOE

(*Calmer now.*) She has the picture albums.

TECOYO

Slow. Slow. Quick-quick.

COYTOE

I've lost children, too.

TECOYO

You still have them, though. It's not the same.

COYTOE

All right. It's not the same.

TECOYO

Don't go back to the burrow.
Stay with me.

They speak as though they have become one another.

COYTOE

You showed me how to follow.

TECOYO

I'm careful with him.

COYTOE

Even the words combed from our mouths have wings
to fly to one another—so graceful—
they flap their little tinfoil wings.

TECOYO

Come with me across the waves.

COYTOE

Not this coyote.

(*Coytoe becomes himself again.*)

I know why a man beats his wife.

TECOYO

Ah! History.
My feet slip back to school.

COYTOE

You talk about being catheterized.
I felt castrated.

TECOYO

Sometimes I graded papers.

Sometimes I danced with Coytoe.
We went Up. Down. Up. Down.
I saw bigger wings growing in place of my little ones.
A mere coyote with open wounds can be wiped clean!

We have loved, Coytoe.
You waited until I was healed.

I would shear myself to bleed there again for you.

You helped me over my loneliness,
but I see there's still two of us—
There's a way we can be one, Coytoe.

(Tecoyo puts her head under the guillotine at the back of her chair.)

I'm sailing west—
The egg of my lovesick heart
in the wicker basket of my ribs.

The guillotine falls with a hiss.

The Toad (Another Name for the Moon) Should Have a Bite

Narrator: Woman in her fifties.

There's no writing on the Great Wall of China.
The Wall of China has no graffiti.
This is my writing on the Wall.

The Great Wall snakes over the mountains along the
northern border of China more than 4,000 miles.

Most of the Wall is impassable.
The Wall is still there, of course, but the top of the Wall
and the walkway on the top are in disrepair.
Over the years, peasants have taken stones from the
Wall to build their houses and outbuildings, their own
little walls.

The elements of weather, the act of disuse, have
crumbled the top of the Wall also. But there has been
reconstruction in places where tourists are allowed.
The armed soldiers tell you where.

I was on a tour bus in China,
and the tour guide told us a story as we traveled:

One year, ten suns appeared in the sky. The land was
cracked and parched. The emperor called his archer,
Hou Yi, to draw his bow and shoot. Nine suns fell.
His reward was a pill of immortality, which his wife
ate. As soon as she swallowed the pill, Chang'e
became light as a toad and hopped to the moon. But
afterwards, she could not return. Often, Hou Yi stood
looking at the moon, where his wife had gone to seek
her own world.

I thought about the husband I left many years ago.
I thought about the life I live on the moon—
when I am riding on a tour bus in China full of people
in evening traffic on the longest street, named
Everlasting Peace.

You go on after your life changes, yet are pulled back.
Memory is an armed guard who tells you where
you go.

In the market, I looked at jade rabbits, paper cranes,
silk jackets, pearls, and a pair of shoes for bound feet.

There was feudal China.

Since the tenth century, women bound their feet to
give them a chance, a way out of poverty. Only a
woman with bound feet could be a courtesan. Her
other choice was to be the wife of a peasant, to be
beaten by a mother-in-law and husband, a life of
cruelty, hard work, and misery.

It wasn't the feudal lord who bound a girl's feet when
she was four or five years old. It was the mother binding her daughter's feet, beating the daughter to get
her to walk, bending the toes under the foot, bowing
the arch.

It's easier to tunnel through the earth, to come out on
the other side and say it is dark here, while we have
the light.

There is no writing on the Wall of China.
Later I talked to someone who had ridden a train
through rural China. *There had been graffiti there,* he
said, *in other places.*

But at the Great Wall, all writing is kept out of sight.
No, maybe not even there. I heard no curiosity, no
questions from the Chinese.
I heard no conjecture. Nothing that indicated
imagination.

Do the Chinese dream at night?
Are their dreams bound like feet?
What is it like to have imagination you can't get to,
though you ride your stout and wooly Mongolian
horse 4,000 miles?
Imagination is not practical, someone said.
But where is the individual who defeated the army
tank in Tian'anmen Square?

The lily slipper measures three inches. It is made of
silk, embellished with gold thread in patterns of flowers and clouds, having the effect of lifting the feet from
the ground.
What pain it takes to separate from the earth.
Strips of cloth wrapped the foot to stunt its growth.
What force of restraint—to break the toes, bend the
bone.

The bound feet must have throbbed with pain—
Often, men would cuddle the woman's feet before
lovemaking—
How close—the pulse of love to hurt?

Where are the cries of the young girls?
Hidden in folds of silence?
Their voice is wind against your face, something you
can feel, but cannot see.

When the moon is a half—a quarter—does Chang'e
walk on bound feet?

The Great Wall of China is made with a facing of brick
and granite stone, filled with earth and fortified every
one hundred yards with a guard post. You see the wall
continue across the mountains from where you stand.

Two hundred years before the birth of Christ, the
Chinese built the Wall on their northern border in
seven years.

Look at me. I am bound.
Let my silence and plainness speak like the Wall of
China.

Like Chang'e, Eve chose her own will—when she had
been told—what? Not to seek her own paradise.

For a week in China, we boarded the bus, we walked,
we rode the boat across the lagoon at the Summer
Palace.
We went through the Forbidden City in Beijing.
We saw the terra cotta warriors near Xi'an.
We had a dumpling dinner.

China came back with me in my dreams.

Little bound feet like birds.
Lily slippers.
Lotus shoes.
Moon shoes—

This little bound foot of a story.

This uneven—this steep walk—
this Great Wall of China—this moon.

Night after night, I carried China with me.
My sleep was another tour through China.

The bound foot, even when unbound, stays bent.
It can never be put back.
I could not go back and live with my former husband,
even though I have no one now.

Is that what love is?
A Forbidden City where no one should be allowed?
When he looked at the moon, did Hou Yi, the archer,
long for Chang'e, his wife, or for his immortality?

In a Chinese theater we saw a man rowing a boat. His
passenger was a woman.
The man held no oar, but he made it look like he did.
There was no boat on the stage, but the man and

woman *seesawed* as the boat turned in the water, moving up and down as the front and back would rise and fall in the waves.
They made us see what was not there.
And what did we not see that was?

I write on the Wall of China to keep the Mongolians out.
Maybe writing itself is a wall.

There are walls in the Old Testament: Jericho and Jerusalem.
In the New Testament, it seems the heavenly city itself is walled.

In the Bible, there is writing on a wall:
You are weighed in the balances, and found wanting.
Daniel, fifth chapter.
But the Chinese killed the missionaries to keep those stories out.

I am found wanting.

I licked words off my wall—the vows of a marriage.
I chose the moon.

I looked at the people on the tour bus, in our seats, egg-cartoned together.
The everlasting traffic.
There's always a haze over the city. There is dirt, squalor.
It's like looking through a dingy window that can never be cleaned.

From the bus, I saw small cars and bicycles everywhere.
Crates of chickens.
A truckload of sheep.
I saw a horse hitched to a small wagon by the street. I saw his dull black eye, the hoof he held up.

Another morning, at dawn, while I was still in my room, I watched the three-wheeled bicycles peddle

their bowls of rice to sell to workers floating over the
streets like fish. One bicycle bumped another, fell back,
caught up, bumped again.
I looked down from my window I could cover with
my thumb if I stood back far enough.

The sun is a lone dictator in the dusty air.

The sky was full of—sky, the sidewalks full of peddlers,
the hawkers full of wares as they went after the tourists
with their bags, their cameras, their weight.

Under the heart is a thorn. You feel it in the night
while traveling in another land
disconnected from what you own, away from your
possessions, your house and its rooms, your furniture.
You sleep with a suitcase between you and the noth-
ingness you are on this earth.

But, unlike Chang'e, you hold a passport that gets you
back.

On the night of the Autumn Festival, when the moon
is bright, the Chinese make small white cakes shaped
like the moon.

The toad is another name for the moon—because the
full moon is speckled or mottled as a toad's back.

I pulled the moon on a string behind me.

I built a wall against the barbarians in myself.

Look at Chang'e on the moon. She is so distant you
can share the loneliness of her reflected light.
You can fall into her craters.

Sometimes you long for something you can't explain.

In the Autumn Festival, the Chinese eat cakes shaped
like the moon.

The toad should have a bite.

Further (Farther)
Creating Dialogue to Talk about Native American Plays

SCENE 1

There has been conversation (at various conferences) toward making a literary theory for Native American plays in which often the unseen world intrudes as though it were seen. The parts not connecting until the play as a whole is seen and sometimes it (the meaning) still trails.

A script is a blueprint for a story that the character enters. Or a character which the story enters. A story wants something but something gets in the way. How it is resolved is the character.

A play connects to a power source which is a structure of action. A cord into a socket. Dramatic language is like electricity. Which is hard to explain. It accesses invisibility and all those things going to it. A play is a small town. With an interstate bypassing it. Yet connected to the power plant by the river. A new oral tradition with breath that is the condition of performance. A planet of being. A location. A vectoring that is a conflation of crossroads in different perspectives.

A Native play is maybe less constructed. Relying at times on campfire or lights from a trailer on the edge of darkness. Not moving to a clear finish with all kinds of imperatives, those little divisions between the spruce and the pines. But accessing the spirit world and the physical world. Combining the shadow world and the real world. Asking which is which? Is the shadow world the spirit world and the real world the physical world we live in? Or is the shadow world the real and the real world we live in the shadow? Or are both distorted until it only seems they are separate?

It is something like magic realism, but we have to invent Native terms.

Improbable realities.

Realized improbabilities.

Improbable actualities.

Ritualistic imagination.

Imaginative realism.

(On a plane from Albuquerque, once it was over Minnesota, I looked down on frozen lakes that had been crossed with snowmobiles and trucks pulling ice-fishing houses. I saw patterns marking the ice with hatchings that looked like broken glass.)

A story in the process of theory.

What is similar and what is not (this came while waking from a dream).

Trying out terms.

Bulling a bulldozer.

A snowmobile on a frozen lake that is only sometimes frozen.

Oneiric magnetism.

A pull of boundaries into one another.

Accessible dualism.

Dualistic accessibility.

Dualistic realism.

Naturalistic dualism (except there are more than two things going on in a Native play; it's more of a bricolage, a staging of variants).

Boundary crossing (so that what is separated on a map—the definite lines between states, for instance, are not there when you look down—but being on the ground, there are only highway markers saying, *Entering Iowa,* but otherwise the borders are invisible unless the Red River between Texas and Oklahoma).

SCENE 2

There is a going into a world that is not the travel you're accustomed to. It exists side by side but is not known. Unless to those within it. It could be said *here it is* without explanation. But there has to be a way to look at. Otherwise, what is it? Emphasis of story over character development? A change of story? The story as character or the telling of the story as character?

Or, if you are there at a certain time / a certain place / it becomes visible like broken glass travels over ice.

Blended settings.

Unboundaried orations.

Seismic *orflations* (inflated orations).

Syncretic *ortations* (each speaking within each).

A dramatic, oral-traditional, many-voiced, poly-multiple, *multipole.*

A play that migrates around ceremony, including the time of year / the elements (a snowmobile on a frozen lake that is only sometimes frozen, depending on the weather) / the particular occasion / the particular voices that give *line.*

A confluence.

A collusion.

When I see the word, petroglyphography, I think of verbal petroglyph.

Voice writing (which a Native play is).

Overlay (not where is the conflict/resolution? character change? but process unfolding the storytelling is the plot).

A dialogue coming from different places. A dialogue without hearing the other (something else from a dream).

Implausible realities.

The believable occurrences of *unbelievability.*

Access to the unseen world(s).

A cohabitation of this world and the other(s) (but without making unrealistic separations). Or *here are other worlds also which are here.*

Intertextual facings.

Interfactual *textings.*

Interfactings.

Overstories.

Understories.

The intermix of overlaps.

The intercalation of (1) the physical world, (2) the dream world (2a those dreams also while waking), (3) the spirit beings (3a the *spirits being*), (4) the ancestors (ancients), (5) the imaginative experience, which is a strip of all between.

SCENE 3

It's when the voices, no matter where they're from, speak outward from the core of experiences, from thought; feeling their way along the dark road to—well, be dramatic about it.

The voices of a longer story. One buffalo walking, overspilling its prairie. Nor do there seem to be soldiers anymore with regiments moving to orders; but a process of exchange, relationship, and interaction; the one voice in many voices, the successive voices, the cumulative voices in manifold expressionism; moving to a fragmented cognizance; a recognition of self in the cross-genre democracy of writing; taking the tool, turning it back to them with new knifeness.

Authority tied in a spiderweb effect, if you've ever watched frost grow. A winter approach to spiderwebs; some garnering a gnat or insect from time to time.

Explications inward of our destination to civilization in these various combinations; a town hall of all of the voices together.

An expanding theory with various centers of the universe, taking in more than one view, more than one multiplicity. The common pervades and speaks the common in a new broken commonality, obedient to the call of changing, manifolding, powwowing, renewing, conviving. Incongruent to get at the matter of the things. To gist existence, all the while sharing the burden, the glory of the stage.

And in the separations, the sewings of meaning again, the contact, at last, with other tribes, other settlements.

DENOUEMENT

A Native play is often orbiculate. To circle back to terms: realized improbabilities probably describes the network of possibilities for the unlikely elements of the topography of the Native stage. The improbable happenings that fill the Native stage. The acceptable improbabilities. The indirect directions. Blizzard, the cold and heat, thunderstorm, humidity, humor and bleakness, tornado and calm, flood and drought—all the other upheavals of Native theater.

Performance Notes and Acknowledgments

The Woman Who Was a Red Deer Dressed for the Deer Dance

This play was presented at:

- Miami University, Oxford, Ohio, with Becky Howard and Diane Glancy, April 8, 2000
- The Birch Wathen Lenox School, 210 East 77th Street, New York City, Marilyn Schulman, Director, November 18–19, 1999
- The Associated Writing Programs Conference, SUNY-Albany, with Anne-E. Wood and Ingrid Lazerwitz, April, 16, 1999
- Raw Space, 529 West 42nd Street, New York City, by The Sage Theatre Company, Barbara Kidd Calvano, Director, with Barbara Kidd Calvano and Alexis Iacono, December 27–30, 1998 and January 2–4, 1999
- The New Dramatists, 424 West 44th Street, New York City, by Mutt Rep, Don Wilson Glenn, Director, with Siouxsan Monson and Barbara Kidd Calvano, September 14, 1995
- The Walker Art Center, Minneapolis, with Diane Glancy and Carolyn Erler, November 11, 1995
- American Indian Community House, 404 Lafayette St., New York City, Siouxsan Monson, Director, with Siouxsan Monson and Margarita Promponas, December 7, 1995

The Woman Who Was a Red Deer Dressed for the Deer Dance was created in part with commissioning support from Walker Art Center, Minneapolis, Minnesota. It was originally published in *XCP2 (Cross Cultural Poetics)*, March 1998; reprinted in *Seventh Generation: An Anthology of Native American Plays*, ed. Mimi Gisolfi D'Aponte (New York: Theatre Communications

Group, 1999), and *Keepers of the Morning Star: An Anthology of Native Women's Theater,* ed. Jaye T. Darby and Stephanie Fitzgerald (Los Angeles: American Indian Studies Press, University of California, Los Angeles, 2001).

The Women Who Loved House Trailers

This play, made possible by a Loft Career Initiative Grant, was presented at The Loft in Minneapolis, October 25, 1996. I am grateful to Jewelle Gomez, Judith Katz, and Leena Kurki, who performed the three women. The fourth character of *The Women Who Loved House Trailers* is the house trailer itself. I wanted to see a multimedia trailer develop during the performance, but I don't have it yet. For the October 25 presentation at The Loft, Jim Turnure put wheels on a birdhouse and used a light to shadow it on the wall.

The piece was read at The American Indian Community House in New York City on September 6, 1996. I am grateful to the Colorado Sisters and Murial Miquel for their reading and comments.

The piece was read at the Cornelia Connelly Center in New York City on February 16, 1998, by Voice and Vision Women's Theater. I am grateful to Melanie Brown, Hortensia Colorado, and Dawn Jamison for reading the parts.

The Women Who Loved House Trailers was presented by Sage Theater Company at Raw Space, 529 West 42nd Street, New York City, on December 27–30, 1998, and January 2–3, 1999. Kim Manion, Amy Beth Sherman, and Amy Soucy played the three women. Barbara Kidd Calvano directed.

I would like to thank Siouxson Monson again for the photographs of Charlie & B. F. Hoover and their house trailer, circa 1932.

I would also like to acknowledge the nine-and-one-half-pound *The Great Bear,* edited by Lauri Honko, Senni Timonen, and Michael Branch, translated by Keith Bosley, Finnish Literature Society Editions, 1993.

American Gypsy

Acknowledgment is due to a Many Voices Fellowship, Playwrights' Center, Minneapolis, during the course of which this play was read on May 27, 2001. Tazra Bryant, Aditi Kapil, Sophie Liu, Shawn Hamilton, Simon Abou-Fadil, and Daniel Cariaga were the readers.

I am most grateful to Jim Turnure for his comments.

Jump Kiss

This play won the Second Annual New Play Competition at the Center for the Performing Arts in Minneapolis, Minnesota. It was presented October 19, 1997, at the Showcase.

Jump Kiss was performed by Sage Theatre Company at Raw Space in New York City, January 23–24, 1999, by Barbara Kidd Calvano, Vera E. Chazen, Vonder Gray, and Louise Martin.

The play was presented as a staged reading at Miami University, Oxford, Ohio, April 8, 2000. Becky Howard was the reader.

Jump Kiss was presented at A Continent of Stories, Native Voices, at the Autry 2001 Play Festival in the Wells Fargo Theater at the Autry Museum for Western Heritage in Los Angeles, March 10, 2001. I am grateful to Randy Reinholz and Jean Bruce Scott, directors of Native Voices.

Dolores Apollonia Chavez, Director and Narrator
Gil Birmingham, Father
Patricia Biggi, Mother
Nathan Chasing Horse, Brother
Tonantzin Carmelo, Sister
Amy Handlesman, Dramaturge
Les Miller, Directing Intern

In the working notes, I stated that the seven plates were "movable and could be read in different order." But the director, Dolores Chavez, moved the pieces around within the plates, leaving the plate numbers as they were. This version of *Jump*

Kiss is the March 2001, Autry one. The Autry performance also included the father and brother. Sometimes Chavez had several characters reading the different lines within one piece. The two male actors, Birmingham and Chasing Horse, played drum, flute, and guitar behind certain pieces: a guitar for *Moving the Grandparents from the Farm,* an Indian drum for *Lung,* and an Indian flute for *Divorce.*

Other possibilites emerged during rehearsal: the voices of the actors. During breaks, the actors told their own stories. The cast was Native, and there was discussion of traditional and Christian ways. It might be possible to extend the performance to include the audience, having small discussion groups afterwards for storytelling. As we talked about the play, everyone involved wanted to tell their own stories. At the discussion with the audience following the Autry performance—which centered around how the play worked for them—the same thing happened. The stories in *Jump Kiss* involved everyone in their own stories, and those stories caused other stories—

Original table of contents:

The Stockyards
Fragment (Back in the house)
Their Graves
Northwest Link Flight #3220, Minneapolis-Lincoln
Downwind, Father

PLATE IV
Divorce
Miscarriage
Fragment (I have a rock)
Dancing Man
Fragment (In this rock snow is falling)

PLATE V
Cold
Lung
Fragment (see Christ going up the ramp)
Street Crud
Fragment (I needed it so)

PLATE VI
My Ears Tuned to the Spirit Realm
Fragment (Sometimes when I bring a
new rock home)
The Clearing
Photo
The Explanation Tale
Fragment (He should have been a vacuum
cleaner salesman)
Rock Concert
When Clouds Were Suds
A Preliminary Moses

PLATE VII
Setting
Head Binding
Glow-ree
Lima Beans

(*Lima Beans,* omitted in the Autry performance:

7:00 a.m. West on Interstate 90. *Welcome to Pennsylvania. America starts here.* I'm on a journey from Upstate New York back to Minnesota.

8:00 a.m. I'm already thinking of lunch. Highway patrol from the other way and I'm twelve miles over.

8:30 a.m.   States are flying by. I'm on a run now from Cleveland to Toledo.

12:16 p.m. Indiana. My map isn't detailed enough to show how to get around Chicago. I fuss with the spirit world, which at one point says, *shut up.* I move on my own and take the wrong turn.

2:06 p.m.   Yessir, right ahead is the slowdown of traffic. The interstate dead-stopped. I'm crawling past Chicago. All this country and one narrow passage through it.

3:30 p.m. I've been on the road since 6:00 a.m. At least I don't need gas. At least it's not ninety-five degrees. At least my car is running.

4:15 p.m.   Traffic moving thirty-five miles an hour then stopped again. Finally, there's Chicago in my rearview mirror, looking something like the cliff dwellings at Mesa Verde.)

> Jump Kiss
> Too Bad He Didn't Know What He Had
> Chicken Load

(*Chicken Load,* omitted in the Autry performance:

On a flight from Birmingham to Atlanta, I hear them loading chickens. I hear the rooster. In front of me a salesman in his white shirt, a plastic cup in his mouth, puts his coat in the overhead storage bin. *You didn't think I could do that without spilling, did you?* he asks.

I think of the brain of a chicken against a DC4 or whatever the plane is.

There's some company, the salesman says, *Tyson*, and they ship chickens for breeding because that's how the world works. He has to know everything, you see. Someone who hasn't succeeded at what he wanted to do. But acts like he has.

Yes, there's chickens on board, the pilot announces. When the engines start, they'll drown out the rooster in the forward luggage compartment who is crowing, crowing, and the people laughing because of the incongruity of his noise, but it was because of his fear that he cawed out again and again, you see, or maybe by then the door was closed and the luggage compartment was dark, and the salesman riding on top of the world was taking his seat.

And what of the chickens and the rooster in the noise of the engine as the plane leaves the ground? Without the insulation of a pressurized cabin? What does it sound like down there in the forward luggage compartment? Do their ears pop in the unpressurized compartment? Is it cold at high altitudes?

The salesman talks to the couple beside him. They're on their way to Bermuda. And the sweet girl beside me in the sixth grade, going to spend the summer with her father, watches me, noticing the hairs on my lip, under my nose, who knows where else, on our way to Atlanta above the rooster flying higher than on his own wings and maybe crowing no longer because of the noise, or the fear that sends him, at last, into silence.

It's always the same. The stronger over the weaker. The jokes about chickens riding in the plane. *Yes, there're two more in the cockpit*, a flight attendant says.

The salesman say he's in pharmaceuticals. The woman says she had to leave her seven-year-old with chicken pox, and the salesman talks about miligrams, doses, even the chicken pox vaccine.

And what are the chickens doing when the planes get backed up and we circle Atlanta while others land, and the salesman uses his authority to be kind, and we're grateful because we know how it can really be, how he could blow us out of the creek with his power?

And the rooster is finding out what real flight is, and the baggage compartment we are loaded into the moment we enter life.

The rooster himself confronting powerlessness in the hen yard.

The pharmaceutical salesman talks about his wife, calling her by her first name in front of the couple he has just met to show them how they are, yes, now friends on this short flight, and he is powerful enough to give them insight into his personal life. He will give them that, yes, because he shows them how generous he is to share his life with them. He's talking now in terms of Dimetapp and Robitussin. And how it feels to have authority and glory about you when you're riding over the helpless fowl who have been pushed roughly into the dark at the end of their world.

Ah! The man is a doctor. The pharmaceutical salesman's telling him how the stockholder decides in short terms what they do as a company. He calls it *the little old lady* syndrome. They want return on their stock investment, and it's probably the best way for the Tyson Company to send chickens and the rooster. Yes, the plane is the quickest way. Expedient and a matter of choice, and how civilized we feel as we ride over the squawking roosters of the world.

But now the plane's landing is delayed, and we circle the Atlanta airport.

And what do you do with these dilemmas for which answers don't come? And how in spite of it, we smile—the sixth-grade girl and I—and now she's marking on her canvas shoes.

And the plane circles the airport for another half an hour, and now it's on its way to the ground with the passengers and the load of chickens and the rooster.

At the gate there is no sound from their compartment. No one mentions them. We gather our belongings and wait in the aisle. Ahead of me the pharmaceutical salesman wishes the doctor and his wife a good trip to a place we know he's already been. Below us, we feel the jolt as the door to the forward luggage compartment is opened. When our door opens, we file out. And whoever is left alive is pulled into the air.)

On November 4, 2001, *Jump Kiss* had a second reading/ development at the Autry Museum in Los Angeles. Once again, the pieces were moved across the plates. The play, originally written as a one-voice piece, which developed into a four, then five-voice piece in the March 2001, reading, became a seven-voice piece by the November 2001, reading. The voices of Husband and Son were added. Slides from old family photographs were used. Guitar, banjo, harmonica, and gourd rattles were added to drum and flute.

> Randy Reinholz, Native Voices Artistic Director
> Jean Bruce Scott, Native Voices Executive Director
> Dolores Chavez, Narrator
> DeLanna Studi, Sister
> Alex Rice, Mother
> Andrew Roa, Father
> Nathan Chasing Horse, Brother
> Michael Wise, Husband
> Brian Wescott, Son
> Elizabeth Bennett, Dramaturg

The following pieces were added:

Mixed Heritage (Father's voice)

How do you forget your voice? How do you fit two worlds together that don't fit? By ignoring the one you are and going with the other. Forgetting your voice. Forgetting your Indian past. You take the lighter way. But in the night, you feel the darkness.

Fragment (Husband's voice)

I married her and now we are together. What do we have to do with one another? She looks one way. I look another.

I open my mouth. Nothing comes. What could I say? Muscular words I have to push down.
What is the function of the heart?

A third piece was added, a poem, "Without Title," from my collection of poems, *Iron Woman*, and one of the actors sang a buffalo song before the piece.

Buffalo Song

It's hard you know without the buffalo,
the shaman, the arrow,
but my Father went out each day to hunt
as though he had them.
He worked in the stockyards.
All his life he brought us meat.
No one marked his first kill,
no one sang his buffalo song.
Without a vision he had migrated to the city
and went to work in the packing house.
When he brought home his horns and hides
my mother said
get rid of them
I remember the animal tracks of his car
backing out the drive in snow and mud,
the aerial on his old car waving
like a bow string.
I remember the silence of his lost power,
the red buffalo painted on his chest.
Oh, I couldn't see it, but it was there,
and in the night I heard his buffalo grunts
like a snore.

The November 4, 2001, table of contents:

PLATE I
My Ears Tuned to the Spirit Realm
Northwest Link Flight #3220, Minneapolis-Lincoln
Characters
Glow-ree
Mixed Heritage
Photo
When Clouds Were Suds
My Composition on Rocks
Galoshes
Downwind, Father
Cold

PLATE II
Setting
Birdlime
A Greater Oven
Head Binding
The Cherokee Strawberry Legend
Buffalo Song
The Stockyards
Credo
Fragment (See Christ going up the ramp.)
Fragment (I needed it so. Forgiveness.)
Fragment (The stockyards where my father worked
    had wooden floors.)

PLATE III
Moving the Grandparents from the Farm
Fragment (I have a rock)
Scars
An Explanation Tale
Vacation Bible School

PLATE IV
Etiology
Lung
Jump Kiss
A Preliminary Moses
Fragment (Back in the house again)

PLATE V

Too Bad He Didn't Know What He Had
Fragment (I married her and now we are together.)
Street Crud
Divorce
Miscarriage
Fragment (I never hired her but she was there
    as mother.)
Fragment (Sometimes when I bring a new
    rock home)

PLATE VI

A Place between Two Trees
The Clearing
Death Bed
Tattoo
Fragment (AAAOOOOHHHH)

PLATE VII

The Piece of Red Licorice
Rock Concert
Their Graves
Dancing Man
There Has To Be Something About Reconciliation
Fragment (In this rock snow is falling.)
Fragment (There are pines in the cemetery.)
My Ears Tuned to the Spirit Realm

In the discussion with the audience after the play, I said I had taken my mother's photographs, turned them into negatives, using the frosty essence and the darkness of a negative, to fill in the events and emotions behind the photos.

I am grateful to the Autry Museum of Western Heritage and to Scott Kratz, Assistant Director of Education at the Autry.

The Lesser Wars

This play was produced during the Sky Woman Festival by Voice and Vision Theater in conjunction with Red Road

Productions at the Henry Street Settlement, Abrons Arts Center, New York City, November 18–21, 1999, Renee Phillippi director, Robert Salas and Amy Tall Chief, actors.

I would like to acknowledge Merril Jordahl for his insight into the vascetomy, for the male perspective after divorce, and for his other words.

Acknowledgments are also due to a Jones Commission from the Playwrights' Center, Minneapolis, during the course of which this play was written.

The Toad (Another Name for the Moon) Should Have a Bite

I was interested in the trip to China because of the Bering Strait link—the possibility the Native American migrated across—

It also was the pain of women—the hurt and distance in gender relations—the absence of romantic love in both cultures.

In reading *The Chinese Conception of the Theatre*, Tao-Ching Hsu, University of Washington Press, 1985, I found some interesting comments on the closeness of [Chinese] drama and poetry, which are often "more of a recital of a narrative poem . . . than a drama" (page 119).

This is also true (sometimes) of Native theater and its reliance on oral tradition.

Another note in the same: "Some of the plays in classical [Chinese] theatre are not dramas but dances. They are usually without any plot and scarcely connected with any story. For example, one such play, *Ch'ang O's Flight to the Moon*, although based on the myth of an ancient archer whose wife took his magic pill, became a goddess and was chased by him to the moon, is, as performed, a solo dance by the goddess without any dramatic action" (page 115).

The interesting point, in this version, is that she was chased to the moon and did not go of her own accord.

I am grateful to Macalester College for supporting my trip to China, October 6–16, 2000.

I would like to thank my colleague, Wang Ping, and her book, *Aching for Beauty, Footbinding in China,* University of Minnesota Press, Minneapolis, 2000.

Thanks are also due to *Cultural Background of China's Folk Customs,* ed. Hu Zong-feng, Northwest University, Xi'an, China, for the story of Chang'e.

The Toad (Another Name for the Moon) Should Have a Bite was first performed at the Flatbush Library, Brooklyn, New York, January 24, 2001, by Naomi Thornton.

The play was read by the author at Birch Bark Books, Gagiigado Series, in Minneapolis, March 15, 2001.

St Paul Pioneer Press, International Briefing
Friday, January 19, 2001
"Tiananmen Figure Freed"

(Beijing) A jailed leader of China's 1989 pro-democracy student protests in Tiananmen Square has been released early from an 18-year-sentence, a human rights group said Thursday, a move it called an attempt to improve its image in a bid to host the 2008 Olympic games. Zhang Jie's family was informed Tuesday that the remaining 6 years of his sentence were being struck, the Hong Kong-based Information Center for Human Rights and Democracy said.

Further (Farther): Creating Dialogue to Talk about Native American Plays

Early versions of "Further (Farther): Creating Dialogue to Talk about Native American Plays" were published in *SAIL (Studies in American Indian Literature)* 11, no. 1 (spring 1999), and in *Journal of Dramatic Theory and Criticism* 14, no. 1 (fall 1999).